JOHN HENRY NASH

The Biography of a Career

Dr. John Henry Nash, a portrait by H. Raschen.

JOHN HENRY NASH

The Biography of a Career

BY

ROBERT D. HARLAN

UNIVERSITY OF CALIFORNIA PRESS
BERKELEY · LOS ANGELES · LONDON
1970

University of California Publications

LIBRARIANSHIP: 7

University of California Press
Berkeley and Los Angeles
California

University of California Press, Ltd.
London, England

ISBN: 0-520-01712-9 (clothbound edition)
ISBN: 0-520-09210-4 (paperback edition)
Library of Congress Catalog Card No.: 70-628359
© 1970 by the Regents of the University of California
Printed in the United States of America

To
My Father
and
The Memory of My Mother

CONTENTS

PREFACE

THIS STUDY is a biography of the career of an important fine printer and a contribution to the history of the fine printing movement in San Francisco. Although both topics are worthy of scholarly investigation, little has been done. Existing studies of Nash consist almost entirely of excessively laudatory articles written during the height of his popularity. Almost nothing has been published, although much has been said, about Nash since his death twenty-one years ago. This long neglect is a striking contrast to the attention Nash commanded in the preceding years, for his work is as underpraised today as it was overpraised during his lifetime. Nash was not *the* fine printing movement in San Francisco, as many of his contemporaries thought. On the other hand, no serious study of this movement can exclude him or ignore his importance. This work attempts to provide a much needed reappraisal of Nash.

San Francisco has been a center of fine printing for over half a century, providing support and a receptive milieu to several competent and a few exceptional men who have seen the trade of printing as the art of fine printing. It has also been a bookish city, encouraging local authors and bookseller-publishers as well as fine printers. Isolated from the great publishing centers in the East, it has nourished local traditions in arts and letters and has enabled its bookmakers to develop interesting and occasionally unique forms of expression. This they have done with some distinction. Yet, except for a few articles, no contributions have been made to the history of a significant movement. It is hoped this Nash biography will be the first of a series of studies of individual firms to be completed in preparation for a comprehensive general history. The series would consider such printing firms as Edward Bosqui, Charles A. Murdock, Taylor and Taylor, the Tomoyé Press, and the several presses which came into being from the twenties to the sixties, and at least these booksellers and publishers: Anton Roman, William Doxey, A. M. Robertson, John Newbegin, and particularly Paul Elder and John Howell.

One reason for my choice of John Henry Nash as the subject of this study has been the close proximity of the Nash Archives to my office, for both are located in the same building. A more compelling reason is the very existence of the Archives, for the records of few of the previously mentioned names have been preserved or are known to have been preserved, and of these firms, except presumably those still in business, only the papers of Taylor and Taylor are as complete as the Nash Archives. Still another reason for my choice was the length, the time, and the significance of Nash's career. He worked in San Francisco from 1895 to 1938, a period which saw the childhood, adolescence, and coming of age of its fine printing movement, and during these years Nash was associated with seven printing firms other than his own, three of which played significant roles in the San Francisco fine printing movement. This study, then, in addition to presenting a comprehensive work on the career of John Henry Nash, makes a contribution as well to histories of these other firms and provides a general setting for the period. Finally, I chose Nash because the time seemed particularly right to undertake a reappraisal of his career.

No complete bibliography of the more than 1,200 Nash imprints exists, and none is provided with this study. Such a bibliography is in preparation by the author. In the meantime, partial listings of Nash's printings can be found in Nell O'Day, *A Catalogue of Books Printed by John Henry Nash* (San Francisco: John Henry Nash, 1937); Martin Schmitt, "John Henry Nash at the University of Oregon," *PNLA Quarterly*, XIII (July, 1949), pp. 129–132; and Charles Evans, "John Henry Nash: the Last Ten Years," *California Librarian*, XXIII (July, 1962), pp. 139–143; 159.

This study proceeds chronologically with two exceptions: Chapter IV (The Twenties) while externally chronological is internally topical, identifying the sources of Nash's success, and Chapter VIII (An Appraisal) presents my conclusions about the significance of Nash's entire career. The "Selected Bibliography" lists the works used in the preparation of this study. An Appendix provides a description of the Nash Archives and Library.

So much of the manuscript material cited in this study is in the Nash Archives that the following rule has been made to avoid unnecessary repetition in the footnotes: when *no* location is given for a manuscript item it is in the Nash Archives.

I wish to thank the following persons who read this work in manuscript for their invaluable criticism: my colleagues, Professor Fredric J. Mosher and Mr. Roger Levenson of the School of Librarianship, and Professor James D. Hart of the Department of English; Messrs. Lawton Kennedy and Oscar Lewis, who knew Nash personally and each of whom has been an important part of San Francisco's fine printing movement for over forty years; Warren Howell, Glen and Muir Dawson, and Donald J. Coombs; and my research assistants Miss Mary Louise Elder and Mr. Carol L. Adams. The cooperation of these persons is also gratefully acknowledged: the University Librarian of the University of California at Berkeley for permission to quote from material in the Nash, Atherton, and Newton-Heron Archives, and from interviews in the Regional Oral History Office; Mr. George Harding, Honorary Curator of the Kemble Collections of the California Historical Society, for permission to use material in the Taylor and Taylor Archives; the Directors of the Book Club of California for permission to quote from the Archives of the Club; Mrs. Weldon C. Nichols, the daughter of John Henry Nash; Mr. George Palé, the residuary legatee of the William Andrews Clark, Jr., estate; Messrs. William E. Conway, Robert G. Cowan, Kenneth A. Lohft, Ward Ritchie, and Dr. Robert L. Leslie; Mrs. Dorothy Whitnah, Executive-Secretary of the Book Club of California; the staffs of the Regional Oral History Office and Rare Books and Special Collections of the University of California; Charles Scribner's Sons; and the publishers of the *Inland Printer* and *Saturday Review*.

CHAPTER I
BEGINNINGS

JOHN HENRY NASH was born on March 12, 1871, in Woodbridge, Ontario, Canada. His father wanted the boy to follow in his footsteps by becoming a mechanical engineer. Accordingly, at the age of sixteen, the young Nash was withdrawn from public school and placed in a foundry where his practical education was to begin. Nash thought his father's choice of occupation a poor one. He wanted to become a printer and threatened to run away from home if his father did not accede to his wishes. The elder Nash capitulated and John Henry was apprenticed to the Toronto printing firm of James Murray and Company in 1888.[1]

Toronto was hardly a center of fine printing at this time, but it was a major printing center of Canada, supporting a variety of newspapers, book, and job firms. Among the largest[2] and best[3] of these was James Murray and Company.

The amount and effectiveness of the training which an apprentice in the printing trade received at that time depended entirely on the disposition and skill of his employer. In James Murray, Nash had a well-disposed and highly skilled teacher who saw to it that his apprentice was thoroughly trained in the mysteries of composition.[4]

Nash's determination, his father's generosity, and Murray's instruction all seemed pointless when, in 1890, Nash abandoned the typecase for the bicycle. He had been caught up in the prevailing rage for bicycle racing which could provide the means for a young man to achieve fame and fortune, two things for which Nash had already developed a decided appetite. For the next two or three years, as a professional racer, he followed the circuit which took him over much of Canada and the United States.[5]

His interest in printing, however, was more enduring, and he returned to the typecase in 1892, in all probability one of the healthiest compositors in the business. Working first for Brough and Caswell, he moved on to another Toronto firm, the Milne-Burgham Company, where he remained until 1894.

Nash left Toronto in the winter of that year. In December he resided briefly in Denver, Colorado, where he took employment with the printing firm of App-Stotts.[6] He remained in Denver for only about four months. Although the "Queen City of the Plains" could offer high wages, thanks to a powerful printing union, it held little else of interest to Nash.

In April, 1895, Nash moved from Denver to San Francisco which was to be his home for the next forty-three years and therefore the site of one of the most colorful careers in the annals of American printing history.

Chapter II

PROBATIONARY PERIOD: 1895–1916

"WEALTHY, EDUCATED, money-spending, pleasure-loving, imbued with the western spirit of success,"[1] San Francisco had enjoyed for several years the kind of reputation which would appeal to the ambitious and adventurous young Nash. Boasting the largest population—some 340,000 persons at the turn of the century—of any city in the United States west of St. Louis, San Francisco could also take pride in its cultural life. Its libraries, though few in number and small in size in comparison to those of other large American cities, were the best in the western United States. Among these, the Mercantile Library was judged by the prestigious Baedeker to be an excellent collection housed in a handsome building,[2] and the Sutro Library which, unfortunately, was to remain in storage for much of this period and much of which was to be destroyed in the earthquake and fire of 1906, was probably one of the finest private collections of incunabula and other early and rare books in the United States at the time. Its historical and scientific societies were active. Its musical and particularly its theatrical seasons were outstanding. The Bohemian Club (est. 1872) was the first of many such clubs to appear in the United States and has been the longest-lived. The Guild of Arts and Crafts, consisting of writers, artists, musicians, architects, and other groups, supported local authors who, in turn, provided material for San Francisco's publishers.

San Francisco was not a great book publishing center of the United States,[3] although firms like Bancroft and Roman were nationally known, but its imaginative and ingenious booksellers and an appreciative clientele certainly made it a bookish center. Among San Francisco's booksellers, William Doxey was the undisputed leader during the 1890's, and his shop in the fashionable Palace Hotel on Market Street was an open window to the literary breezes from the East and from Europe. These breezes were heavily perfumed with the bittersweet aroma of the *fin-de-siècle*. *The Lark*, a fanciful and irreverent little magazine produced by "les Jeunes," a group of local authors and artists, and published by Doxey, was San Francisco's own contribution to the *fin-de-siècle*, and its enthusiastic reception in the eastern United States and even in London added to San Francisco's already colorful image.

A more significant source of this image was San Francisco's decidedly cosmopolitan population which so impressed the American and European visitor. Situated on the Pacific coastline of the United States, San Francisco faced both East and West. To the German, French, Italian, Russian and other European colonies and the Mexicans who contributed to the melting pot were added Filipinos, Hawaiians, and a sizeable Chinese population. The latter's Chinatown quarters added an exotic element not found in many American cities.

Tolerance, as well as vitality, resulted from this ethnic mixture, for San Franciscans had learned generally to live together in harmony. Tolerance encouraged a mutual receptiveness to art in whatever form it assumed, "each race weaving its own bit into the blending tapestry."[4] Art, music, and literature were enriched by this mixture. So also was printing, and it is significant that the first exhibit of books and printing to be held in San Francisco, in January, 1897, was sponsored not by the booktrade but by the Guild of Arts and Crafts.

San Francisco's history added another strong element to the tradition of its printing—opulence. During the 1850's and 1860's, when San Francisco and California enjoyed unusual prosperity, her printers were seldom restricted by conservative tastes or competitive prices. Business was conducted on a lavish scale and demanded equally lavish printing. The printers' excellent profits were invested, in part, in additional type and equipment which, in turn, enabled California's printers to achieve in their work a virtuosity seldom equalled by eastern printers. While this trend was not generally sustained during the last third of the century, which was inaugurated by the economically "terrible Seventies," a tradition of deluxe printing was continued and enriched by the appearance of individual works.

One such work was a handsome duodecimo edition of Bret Harte's *Lost Galleon*, printed and published in 1867 by Towne & Bacon. Three particularly attractive volumes were produced by Edward Bosqui & Company, established in 1863. The first of these, an edition of Charles W. Stoddard's *Poems*, also published in 1867, used woodcuts by the popular artist William Keith. There followed, in 1874, an edition comprising one hundred copies of Father Francisco Palou's *Noticias de la Nueva California* which cost its publisher the substantial amount of $2,000.[5] This publication was cited by the *Inland Printer* as the best single specimen of bookmaking produced up to that time in San Francisco.[6] Three years later, in 1877, the firm printed a folio edition containing full-page colored lithographic plates of *The Grapes and Grape Vines of California*. This work was displayed at the Paris Exposition, held that same year, where it received warm praise.[7] The Bosqui firm deserved these rewards, for its best bookmaking was equal to that produced anywhere else at the time. Bosqui's preeminence among San Francisco's printers was unchallenged until the 1890's when, for the first time, his motto "Quality, not quantity" could have been assumed as well by other firms, including, in particular, the E. D. Taylor Company and C. A. Murdock & Company.

San Francisco had produced a tradition for fine printing which was clearly evident by the 1890's. Nash must have been aware of this tradition, and this knowledge may in large part have decided him to travel west rather than east from Denver.

San Francisco's literate, cultured society, her comparative isolation from the publishing centers of the East, and her requirements as a large city for printing in all forms, from substantial books to calling cards and blank forms, demanded a variety and number of printing establishments. Supply often exceeded demand, however, during the economically lean final quarter of the nineteenth century, and the 61, 116, and 180 printers listed for 1880, 1890, and 1900,[8] were often hardpressed to find sufficient orders.

While intellectually and artistically so exciting a period for San Francisco, the 1890's were a particularly difficult decade for the city's printing trade, and 1895, when Nash arrived jobless, was one of the worst years. The severe financial panic of 1893 had become a persistent depression in San Francisco which, unlike other major western cities, seemed unable to recuperate. A strike of printing house employees for a shorter work day of nine hours threatened to destroy what little recovery the printing trade had made from that depression. Two of the city's leading printing firms, Bosqui and

Francis-Valentine, had been burned out on Christmas day of 1893,[9] and were not yet fully rebuilt. The *San Francisco Chronicle* had recently installed seven linotypes, each of which was said to be capable of performing the work of four men, and there was real fear among the compositors of the city that they would be replaced by this infernal machine.

THE HICKS-JUDD COMPANY

The unhealthy state of printing in San Francisco at the time of Nash's arrival would have discouraged an older or less confident man, but Nash was in the prime of his youth and was already a skilled and talented compositor. These assets carried him through, and he soon found employment with the Hicks-Judd Company, one of the largest and best equipped printing establishments on the Pacific coast. Here Nash was employed as a compositor.[10] Unknown, relatively unproven, and probably quite happy to have secured the most routine position, Nash was not singled out by his employers for special attention. But his talent was soon apparent to more discerning eyes. Joseph FauntLeRoy, who was later to be Nash's chief assistant and who at this time was the foreman of the Raveley Printing Company of San Francisco, notes in his biography of Nash that in 1895 there came to his attention a type form of a business card for printing, the workmanship of which, in his opinion, was superior. The compositor was Nash.[11]

THE STANLEY-TAYLOR COMPANY

Nash's second employer, for whom he began work as a compositor sometime in 1898,[12] was a relatively new firm which had, however, already achieved recognition for its attractive printing. The Stanley-Taylor Company was formed in 1898 as an amalgamation of the D. S. Stanley Company, which had been continuously in business in San Francisco since 1878, and the E. D. Taylor Company, established in 1896. Stanley, the senior partner, was among the elders of the printing community, but it was Taylor's drive and enthusiasm which directed the new firm. Edward DeWitt Taylor, a native of San Francisco, was the elder son of the talented Dr. E. R. Taylor—

physician, lawyer, printer, poet, and politician—from whom the boy learned the rudiments of printing. At the age of seventeen, Taylor was made a member of the San Francisco printing union; he proceeded to practice his trade for much of the remainder of his long life. His pronounced and progressive ideas about efficiency and quality in the production of commercial printing were in large measure effected. Following it's establishment in 1896, the E. D. Taylor Company received quick recognition for both skillfully and tastefully executed composition and presswork.[13] This reputation was fully maintained following the merger.

Taylor boasted of his and his staff's thorough knowledge of the history of bookmaking and claimed in an advertisement, with no little exaggeration, that as a result of this exceptional knowledge, Stanley-Taylor "had achieved a success in book-making such as other printers have as yet been unable to achieve."[14] Certainly, no other San Francisco firm at this time was so consciously aware of schools, styles, and trends in printing. The firm was to achieve international fame and reputation within four years of its founding when, in 1902, it was awarded the Gold Medal and Definitive Diploma at an international exhibition held in Rome.[15]

It seems almost inevitable that Nash should find employment with Stanley-Taylor, and that his ability should be appreciated by the discerning Taylor. Nash was soon made a foreman. In this position he had, for the first time, relative freedom to express his own ideas about printing and book design, and this freedom was beneficial to both Nash and his employer. One wonders if Nash's was not the "master-mind" which, in the opinion of the *Inland Printer*, was "directing the disposition and arrangement of the matter to the best advantage."[16]

In 1901, Nash prepared examples of display composition for the first two issues of Stanley-Taylor's new quarterly, the *Western Printer*, that remarkable publication which contains articles by such important persons as Morgan Shepard, Henry R. Plomer, and Charles Jacobi. Nash also designed and set all the advertisements for the first number of this periodical. They are by any standards models of effective and appropriate style; for the time and place of their production, they are minor miracles. However, the cover rather than the contents of this periodical provided Nash with the medium for the expression of his real *tour de force*—the mitered rule. The cover design, an elaborate architectural border, was constructed entirely of brass rule, three hundred and twenty-two miters being made. It remains today a masterpiece of rule work.

The *Western Printer* was merged with the *American Printer* slightly over one year after its first appearance. That its life was as short as it was brilliant suggests that the printing trade in general in the United States and in particular on the West Coast was not yet ready to appreciate and to support a trade journal of its quality and speciality. However, it had given Nash the opportunity to display his talent and to establish the foundations of his reputation.

THE SUNSET PRESS

Nash left Stanley-Taylor for a brief period in 1900 to become the superintendent of the Sunset Press at 106–108 Union Square Avenue.[17] His friend and former colleague of Toronto days, Bruce Brough, was the manager of the firm. Both men probably left the relative security of employment with Stanley-Taylor to find greater financial reward in this organization. The Sunset Press was prepared to accept orders for designing, photography, engraving, and printing and claimed it could do so to advantage, having "the best-equipped Engraving and Printing establishment west of Chicago, with the best facilities—the latest designs in type and finest machinery."[18]

Brough and Nash's ownership of the Sunset Press was short lived; another of their advertisements, which stated that they were "wide-open for business,"[19] describes a condition that was apparently all too real. However, considering the short period of their association with that firm, it is remarkable that they managed to achieve the reputation they did. At least one opinion, that of the reviewer of specimens of printing submitted for review in the *Inland Printer*, was unusually complimentary: "For excellence of design, delicacy of treatment in colors and general effectiveness, the work under review would be hard to equal, much less excel."[20] Flattering reviews do not pay bills; within one year, both Brough and Nash were again on the payroll of Stanley-Taylor.

STANLEY-TAYLOR AGAIN

It was after his return to Stanley-Taylor that Nash executed some of his best work, including his contributions to the *Western Printer* which have already been described. Nash left Stanley-Taylor again in 1901. He was to return to it a third time in a few years. His tenure there from 1898 to 1901 had done his career and his education incalculable good. He had been associated with an employer who appreciated good work and recognized and encouraged Nash's talents. Nash was to be associated again with Edward Taylor, but never again would the impact of Taylor or any other man have so profound an influence upon Nash's career.

Nash was now thirty years old. He had been accorded recognition by one of the city's best printing houses, and, through the *Western Printer*, his work had been introduced to a large and appreciative audience. It would have been no small achievement even for a man half again his age to have examples of his work given such conspicuous display. At the same time, however, he had obtained neither the position nor the financial reward commensurate, in his opinion, with his performance. For these reasons he now attempted to establish his own firm.

THE TWENTIETH CENTURY PRESS

The Twentieth Century Press, named in honor of the newly arrived century, was only half Nash's firm, for he held it in partnership with Bruce Brough. The partners' new venture was advertised as a quality printing house,[21] and they were confident enough about this assertion to advise clients that their best work was to be done when matters of taste were left in their hands.[22] Judging by the six extant examples in Nash's collection of his work, that taste is questionable by our standards. However, a critique in the January, 1903 *American Printer* of other Twentieth Century Press imprints suggests that these examples are of a higher quality than those which have survived. That critique contains this flattering appraisal:

This month it is The Twentieth Century Press, San Francisco, Cal., that gets the prize for the best collection of specimens sent to this journal. As may be expected from this statement, the samples received from The Twentieth

Century Press are of a very high order. They comprise everything from office stationery to bound booklets, each individual piece of printing bearing the stamp of an artist. Not only is the composition of a high order, but the selection of ink and paper admirably supports the work of the composing-room.

It was at this time that Nash began to experiment in earnest with handmade and colored paper, with colored ink, and with striking typographical design. Other characteristics of the fine press were introduced, including elaborate colophons, a printer's mark, and exotic bindings.

Probably just these features attracted the Twentieth Century Press's chief clients, Paul Elder and Morgan Shepard, whose fashionable book and art shop on Post Street was as self-consciously "arty" as was Nash and Brough's press. Both Elder and Shepard were interested in publishing as well as selling books, and they liked the work of the Twentieth Century Press. Additionally, Nash had already done some work for them when he was with Stanley-Taylor. For these reasons they became important clients whom Brough and Nash relied upon heavily.

THE TOMOYÉ PRESS

This dependence caused the simultaneous demise of the Twentieth Century Press and birth of the Tomoyé Press, its successor, in 1903. Elder–Shepard having sold his interest in the firm—wanted an even closer association than had previously existed between printer and publisher. Nash and Brough were eager to cooperate. Elder proposed that the press be called the Tomoyé Press. It was to make a deep and colorful impression upon American fine bookmaking.

Elder's printing needs varied from substantial books to catalogs, calendars, stationery, birthday, Valentine, Easter, and Christmas cards, and a large amount of other ephemera. His publication program favored California authors, whose works ranged in genre from poetry to parody to plays. Elder himself occasionally turned author, or, more exactly, compiler, to produce anthologies. Occasionally he brought out reprints of standard titles, but he preferred works by California authors. He styled himself "A Western Publisher."[23]

His requirements in printing, which kept the Tomoyé Press quite busy, included about a dozen books a year, several pamphlets, and a substantial amount of job work. His requirements in style gave the Tomoyé Press a wide margin for experimentation. Nash was to say several years later that he was in complete charge of the designing as well as the production of the printing which was issued from the Tomoyé Press.[24] It seems equally likely that Elder established the overall style, for he knew exactly what he wanted.

This fact is most apparent in the setting which Elder provided in his shop for the Tomoyé Press books. Inside the shop, *objects d'art,* furniture, and books were intermingled, each contributing to the others' visual appeal. Stained redwood provided a rich background highlighted by leaded glass, and the entire shop was dominated by William Keith's spectacular painting *Upland Pastures.* The books were displayed in this colorful setting on antique tables and in attractive glass cases, along with "exquisite antiques in brass and bronze, choice vases and bits of pottery, with a few well chosen photographs and cards on the walls."[25] Elder's aim, to create in his shop an "uncommon atmosphere,"[26] was fully realized. "Where," one proud San Franciscan asked, "but in San Francisco can one find a bookshop like an asthetic library?"[27] Another equally enthusiastic observer said that Elder's shop was altogether the most attractive in San Francisco outside of Chinatown.[28]

Elder regarded his books, like the pottery, jewelry, and antiques with which they were displayed in his shop, as art objects. The results of this policy, as seen in his publications, occasioned the partially adverse criticism found in the first review in a national printing trade journal of Tomoyé Press items. George French's comments in the May, 1905, issue of the *American Printer,* while praising the workmanship of the Tomoyé Press and even the "scheme" for each book, also noted that there was generally lacking "the surveillance of a purpose guided by those few and simple art principles that are necessary in a book that is made as well as it can be."[29]

It is surprising that the Tomoyé Press books are well made at all, for Elder had very different attitudes towards his shop and Nash's. While generous, even extravagant, in supporting the bookshop, Elder expected maximum effort at minimum costs from the Tomoyé Press. Nash was later to complain that Elder was reluctant to pay even equitable prices. For example, on one book which Nash was producing just before the earthquake and fire of 1906, he was allowed 45¢ a page. When later Nash obtained estimates for the same book from some printers in New York City, the lowest figure he was quoted was $2.15 a page. In March, 1906, the Tomoyé Press failed. Elder advanced Nash $1,000 to keep the press in business,[30] but within a month his own shop was in ruins.

The fire which followed the earthquake of April 18 completely destroyed the commercial section of San Francisco. Not one bookshop or printing plant in that part of the city was spared. Elder was lucky to be able to retrieve a few pieces of jewelry and some records from the shambles of his office. Everything else was gone. The plant of the Tomoyé Press was a complete loss.

Assuming that bravado which most San Franciscans displayed—it was called "the Spirit of '06"—Elder soon commissioned Bernard Maybeck to design new quarters for his bookshop. In the Old English style, with massive beams, a peaked roof, and dormer windows, the shop was located at the corner of Van Ness Avenue and Bush Street, in the heart of San Francisco's temporary new shopping center.

While it was possible to reopen the bookshop, it was not practical at the time to reconstruct the well-equipped printing plant necessary to support Elder's publishing program. In June, therefore, leaving John Howell and Theodore Keane in charge of the new San Francisco shop, Elder joined other San Franciscans in what was for him a reluctant exodus to the East. The publishing headquarters of Paul Elder and Company were reestablished in New York City. The "and Company" included the Tomoyé Press and John Henry Nash, but not Bruce Brough, who severed his connections with the Press at this time.

Elder attempted in New York City to recreate the atmosphere of his San Francisco shop. Located at 43 and 45 East Nineteenth Street the new quarters included an Arts and Crafts Book Room, "a quaint little den" which displayed *objects d'art*, paintings and prints, photographs, jewelry, embroidery, and rare and in-print books, the latter category consisting of "the unique output of the Tomoyé Press."[31]

Elder's taste in the subject and style of his books was not changed by his removal to New York City. He remained primarily a publisher of California authors and western subjects, and most of his books and other imprints, produced by the Tomoyé Press, continued to be unusual in appearance. An exhibit of Tomoyé Press books held in New York City in May, 1907, was favorably reviewed by local critics, one of whom gave the complimentary opinion that Nash must be ranked as one of the great printers of America.[32] The following year Lewis C. Gandy's article "Modern Commercial Typography" contained reproductions of the title pages and sample text pages from *Abelard and Heloise, The Raven,* and *Christmasse Tyde.* The article concluded with the opinion that "in straight typography —that is, with only foundry type and rules—Mr. Nash has achieved results in some ways superior to the draughtsman."[33] Also in 1908, reproductions of the title page and a text page of John De Morgan's *In Lighter Vein* were included in Edmund G. Gress's article on typography in the *American Printer.* Gress's accompanying comments contained high praise for Nash's ability as a typographer.[34] In 1909, Gress selected Nash's printing of an Elder catalogue as an example of the expert use of rule borders in a manner which, he said, went beyond anything the average typographer would have thought possible.[35]

Among Nash's best work done during this period is the 1907 four-volume set of Western Classics, containing Bret Harte's *Tennessee's Partner,* W. H. Rhodes's *The Case of Summerfield,* Robert Louis Stevenson's *The Sea Fogs,* and Ambrose Bierce's *A Son of the Gods* and *A Horseman in the Sky.* The volumes are all printed on handmade Fabriano paper and their format is also uniform, but each volume uses a different typeface and typographical scheme. One employs Caslon 471 and another Bookman; the third is printed in Scotch Roman and the fourth in Cheltenham Wide. The handsomely boxed set has always been a favorite of Nash collectors.

The restraint of this work, which is exceptional for a product of the Tomoyé Press, was not the result of any influence exerted upon Nash by New York City's bookmakers. That great city offered unequalled opportunities for one to study the masterpieces of the past— at the Metropolitan Museum, the Lenox Library, and the Library of the Grolier Club—but at this time it was not a center of fine printing. Probably Nash did not have the time to utilize those opportunities which did exist. He worked, he says, six days a week and frequently eighteen hours a day. He had a wife and infant daughter and probably a commuting problem, since he lived in Flatbush.[36]

However, because Nash was in New York City and not three thousand miles away in San Francisco, he met two men who had a decided influence upon his career. The first of these men was Theodore Lowe DeVinne, the undisputed Nestor of American printers. Nash knew DeVinne's work, had read his four printing treatises, and was properly impressed. Thus when DeVinne asked Nash to call upon him, Nash was delighted. The meeting, which probably took place sometime in 1908, was later described by Nash, who quoted DeVinne as saying:

Mr. Nash, I have sent for you for a certain purpose. Printing has gotten to the point where the only thing we hear is "costs" and "prices" and "costs." We have entirely forgotten the art of printing. Printing was a great major art for 300 years and it was recognized in Venice as the greatest of all the arts. Some one has got to work at printing, and work all their life with their hands in the type case. I am going to ask you to work as long as you live with your hands in the type case.[37]

While Nash may have some of the words wrong, he did comprehend accurately their message—that an artist must work with his hands or cease to be an artist. DeVinne's interest in Nash suggests that he had followed Nash's career closely, that he had studied and been impressed by Nash's work, and that he saw in Nash a potentially excellent printer. The fact that DeVinne had talked to him at all must have strengthened Nash's self-confidence and encouraged his own interest in producing really fine printing.

Nash's other important introduction was to Henry Lewis Bullen, the director of the recently established Typographical Library and Museum of American Type Founders Company (hereafter referred to as ATF) in nearby Jersey City. The collection was not extensive when Nash first met Bullen there, but its very existence must have impressed him. More impressive was Bullen himself, one of the most informed and stimulating printing historians then living in the United States. From their first meeting until Bullen's death several years later, after a long and distinguished career, the two men remained good friends, and Bullen was one of Nash's most ardent and influential advocates.

Nash made other friends in New York City. Among these were F. B. Berry, the Director of ATF, and Thomas N. Fairbanks and P. H. Bancroft of the Japan Paper Company, whose stock Nash had used so effectively and ingeniously at the Tomoyé Press. The offices of the Japan Paper Company were saturated with specimens of Nash's use of its paper; these were shown eagerly to clients and visitors. The Japan Paper Company was to act, in effect, as an advertising agency in New York City for Nash for several years.

By 1909, San Francisco had recovered sufficiently from the earthquake and fire of 1906 for Paul Elder and Company and the Tomoyé Press to be able to return. They were probably happy to do so, for their success in New York City and the East had been only moderate, at best. Elder had remained a publisher primarily of western authors, and his works published in New York City had lost, it was said, much of its intangible western element that had been their charm.[38] The logical setting for Elder's firm was the West. New York City and the East had no apparent influence on either Elder's or Nash's interests and methods. Nash had made the greater impact than Elder upon the New York City booktrade, but while his work had been admired there by some important persons, there was no place in the East for the Tomoyé Press without Paul Elder and Company.

The exiles returned to San Francisco in February, 1909.[39] Shortly thereafter, Elder secured a ten-year lease on the building at 239 Grant Avenue. Again, he turned to the architect Bernard Maybeck to design and decorate the interior of the building in a manner that would create the mood he wanted. Elder's efforts in this direction were apparently more appreciated in San Francisco than in New York City. For example, the *San Francisco Chronicle* was rhapsodic in its description of the new quarters.[40]

The Tomoyé Press, which occupied the third floor of the building, was no longer a complete printing plant, for Nash began farming out his presswork, a practice that was to continue for the remainder of his long career. It was, rather, only a composing room, and the resulting decrease in equipment and personnel allowed Nash, as DeVinne had advised, to set much of his own type and to keep a close watch over every step of the work done in his shop.

Much of this output consisted of calendars, motto cards, catalogs, stationery, and other ephemera, and on its production Nash had to expend most of his time and energy. Nor did the subject matter of the books he printed offer much inspiration. On Elder's author list, local lady poets and compilers predominated. Their works are not remembered.

Nash was given relative artistic freedom in producing these works, and for this reason alone his years with Paul Elder were valuable. To his credit it may be said that the main body of his Tomoyé Press imprints is of high quality. If he was capable of an occasionally excessive imagination in his typographical designs, he was also able to produce work which appealed to such discerning contemporaries as DeVinne, Bullen, George French, and Charles A. Murdock.

In 1910, an exhibit of Tomoyé Press books was held in San Francisco. Nash's work was warmly praised by several critics including the judicious Murdock who had flattering comments for both the artistic and technical skill of Nash.[41] The following year Nash was invited to submit a statement of his aims to the *American Bulletin*. His comment, that "every book or booklet we make is made as carefully as if it represented only one copy for presentation,"[42] reflects that obsession with perfection which had so impressed Murdock and others and which had already removed Nash so far from the mainstream of American printing.

In spite of recognition Nash was dissatisfied with his position, primarily because his salary had not kept pace with his growing reputation. For this reason and others, among which was the incompatibility between the needs of the publisher and the aspirations of the printer, Nash found his relationship with the Tomoyé Press and Paul Elder untenable by mid-1911. His departure from the Tomoyé Press was marked with bitterness and recrimination. Elder and Nash were not on speaking terms for several years.

Nash's work with the Tomoyé Press and Paul Elder and Company had been important to his career. Elder's varied requirements in printing and his interest in the visually striking had allowed Nash an unusual margin for experimentation. Elder's receptiveness to the idea of the book beautiful had enabled Nash to produce much of that work upon which his reputation as a fine printer was based. Elder's standing as a publisher had secured for Nash's work a wide distribution. Elder's removal to New York City from 1906 to 1909 had caused Nash's as well, and while in that city Nash had made important friends. Finally, Elder's success as a dealer of deluxe merchandise had impressed upon Nash the fact that there was a good market in San Francisco and California for fine printing. Through his association with Elder, Nash had been introduced for the first time to quality. He was not to forget the pleasure of its company.

TAYLOR, NASH & TAYLOR

Nash next returned to his former employer the Stanley-Taylor Company. Its aims and methods were quite different from those of Paul Elder. Stanley-Taylor was a commercial printing house whose customers were not primarily the bookstore's but rather a varied group of businessmen and firms. Additionally, Stanley-Taylor seldom assumed the role of publisher. Its standards of workmanship were as high as those of the Tomoyé Press, but its style was almost totally antipathetic. With some exceptions, its products showed few of the ravages of the disease of "Morrismania." Stanley-Taylor's style, distinguished by its austerity, depended for its effect on well-selected paper, types, and ink, on a conservative use of decorations, and on careful, even impeccable, presswork. Finally, the firm made no claims to being exceptional other than in the quality of all its work. It was a commercial printing house, working within the tradition of commercial printing, and prepared to compete with standard prices.

The structure of the firm had changed by the time Nash rejoined it in 1911, D. S. Stanley having sold his interest in 1905, and Henry H. Taylor, the brother of Edward DeWitt, having assumed a prominent role. Both Taylors were skilled printers, effective salesmen, and competent administrators. Each had an interest in and knowledge of the history of printing. Henry, in particular, was to attain a command of the subject which would exceed even that of Nash.

The formation of Taylor, Nash & Taylor, the firm's new name, was an important occurrence within the printing community of San Francisco, for it united three men whose interest in quality printing was exceptional. Nash secured definite advantages in his new position. For the first time, the title of a printing firm with which he was associated bore his name. He was assured a regular salary (this seems not to have been the case with the Tomoyé Press), and given the position of Vice-President, a three years' contract, and the promise at the end of the three years of a one-sixteenth share in the stock interest of the firm. His weekly salary of $57.50[43] was most adequate for the time. Perhaps more important for Nash, he was allowed complete control of the Fine Work Department which had been created especially for him. The only proviso was that his department, like the others in the firm, was expected to show a profit.

One of Nash's first jobs, following his appointment in September, 1911 was to print the announcement of that appointment. It is dated September 28 and says:

The Stanley-Taylor Company takes pleasure in announcing Mr. John Henry Nash is associated with the firm as one of its active members and the change of its corporate name to Taylor, Nash, and Taylor. Mr. Nash will be in charge of the Fine Work Department, to which he brings the wide experience developed during his former connection with this house and more recently with Paul Elder & Company, where, as designer and originator of the beautiful books and leaflets issued by that firm for the five years last past, he has acquired a national reputation as a master craftsman among printers. On the grounds of past performance, and in the reasonable expectation of still higher achievements in the future, the new firm requests your patronage.

This and other work produced in 1911 show a new Nash in the restraint of their typographical design. For the Fine Work Department, the year 1912 was productive. Three items were singled out for praise: Clarence Thomas Urmy's *A California Troubadour*, Charles W. Stoddard's *A Bit of Old China*, and in particular a reprinting of Charles Dickens' *What Christmas Is as We Grow Older*. *Printing Trade News of New York* proclaimed the latter work to be one of the most beautiful pieces of printing that had ever been executed.[44] Nash probably found greater pleasure in the more rational compliment of the discriminating Henry L. Bullen: "there is not even a little fault to be found with it."[45] The signal honor of 1912 for the Fine Work Department, and a personal triumph for Nash, was the appearance in the *Printing Art*, [46] of "Distinctive Typography: An Exhibit of the Work of Taylor, Nash and Taylor. San Francisco, California, U.S.A.," an article containing eight pages of examples of Taylor, Nash & Taylor's work, most of which was Nash's.

Honors accumulated. Nash's 1913 printing of John Galen How-ard's volume of poetry entitled *Brunelleschi* was acclaimed as a masterpiece. It was, said Bullen, whose praise of Nash had become increasingly fluent, "a beautiful example of chaste typography, with all the details of proportion, margins, color and workmanship per-fectly arranged."[47] The firm's Christmas gift for that year, *A Ha! Christmas*, was almost equally successful.

Nash's very significant contributions to the reputation of Taylor, Nash & Taylor reached their peak in December, 1914, and the first months of 1915. During this period, the *TNT Imprint*, "the house-organ preeminent,"[48] was inaugurated. The first issue of this handsome publication, dated December, 1914, contains this state-ment of purpose on page 16:

It is not our intention to issue the TNT Imprint in any stereotyped size or typographic format. Each issue will very likely be printed upon an entirely different paper, of such size as may seem best at the time, and will probably be entirely different in typographic handling. The idea, however, is not to show an excessively elaborate piece of work. Our intention is rather, to keep the publication essentially simple in character, and the type will be set nearly always on the machine. In other words, this little monthly will be an in-expensive, every-day piece of printing, such as you could profitably, and without excessive cost, employ in advertising your own business.

Nothing that Nash had done previously excelled his work on the *TNT Imprint* which was, without doubt, the best house organ the printing community had seen. It made Taylor, Nash & Taylor the talk of the trade.[49]

In later years, when Nash and the Taylors had gone their very separate ways, a tendency developed to negate Nash's contributions to the firm's reputation. While it is true that Taylor and Taylor retained in every respect the high position achieved by Taylor, Nash & Taylor, it must also be said that it is easier to maintain than to achieve reputation. In securing its enviable status, the firm owed much to John Henry Nash, for nearly all of its work which achieved acclaim from 1911 to 1915 came from the Fine Work Department.

As Nash's reputation grew so did his antipathy towards the Tay-lor brothers who he felt did not appreciate him sufficiently. There were other difficulties as well. Nash was not a good orthodox busi-nessman; the Taylors were. Nash was a perfectionist in a line of work where perfection meant substantially increased costs; the Taylors were also perfectionists, but were more willing at the same time to accommodate themselves to practical considerations. Nash's talk about the printer as an artist probably confused Edward DeWitt Taylor; it must certainly have annoyed Henry H. Taylor who was made decidely uncomfortable by such talk. Additionally, Nash felt that he should be allotted a greater financial reward for his significant contributions to the firm's reputation. This, apparently, was not forthcoming. Nash once remarked, perhaps facetiously, that he would have stayed with Taylor, Nash & Taylor if he had had enough money to buy a Ford[50]—his taste for Cadillacs developed later—but he did not get it, and his financial frustrations added to the irritations resulting from the clash of three forceful personalities. Nash left Taylor, Nash & Taylor in April, 1915. The parting was not pleasant. That Nash was not entirely to blame can be seen in the ungracious and ungenerous reference to him in the June *TNT Imprint* in an article entitled "Teamwork Counts," which concluded with these comments:

Occasionally we find a man who can't work in harness, one who gets the idea that he is the whole organization, and that the firm will go smash without him—but this class of man does not last in our plant. He is not slandered, nor abused, nor picked upon—he is eliminated automatically.

BLAIR-MURDOCK COMPANY

In joining the staff of the Blair-Murdock Company, Nash associated himself with one of the few remaining printing houses in San Francisco whose reputation for producing quality printing approached that of his two former employers—the Tomoyé Press and Taylor, Nash & Taylor. By the time Nash joined the firm in 1915, that reputation was based more on past than on present achievements, for Charles A. Murdock had sold his interest in March, and Blair-Murdock, under the poor management of Ralph Kirkman Blair, had already begun its rapid descent to ruin.

Probably to reinforce the new firm's old reputation for quality printing Blair hired Nash. The price was high. Nash was given his own composing room, and he mentions, as well, having been paid $5,000,[51] although whether this money was an outright bonus, or stock, or his salary is not clear. Additionally, Blair was taking a decided risk in bringing into his organization a man whose local reputation for irascibility equalled that for skillful printing.

Blair-Murdock's announcement, proclaiming its pleasure in having secured Nash's services, refers to Nash as one of the foremost printers of America. The less prejudiced *Pacific Printer and Publisher* concurred with this opinion at about the same time. Its opinion is here quoted in full, for it reflects the high regard in which Nash was generally held on the West Coast at the time and why:

John Henry Nash has long held rank well up among the printers of America. He is recognized as a leader in the matter of taste and of technical skill. He developed a distinctive style early in life, and his love for the art has led him to continue the pursuit of the best so that with the passing years he has added to his achievements and kept the lead he took as a young man. Mr. Nash looks upon printing as in reality one of the arts. It is one method of expressing that combined feeling and imaginative quality that marks the highest conceptions. Printing has its business side, but with it is its art side in which its greatest value inheres.[52]

Most of Nash's work for Blair-Murdock was ephemera, books comprising only about one-third of his output. A large part of this material, in all categories, pertained to the Panama-Pacific International Exposition which dominated San Francisco's social and economic life from 1912 to 1916. Held from February 20 to December 4, 1915, the Exposition commemorated the completion of the Panama Canal and celebrated the reconstruction of San Francisco from the earthquake and fire of 1906. The Exposition's extensive advertising program required substantial printing and publishing, some of which was commissioned from local firms.

Blair-Murdock obtained a generous share of this work and was even given the impressive title of "Printer of the Panama-Pacific International Exposition Official Guide Book." While Nash was not involved in the production of this publication, he did design and supervise the printing for the Exposition officials of several broadside certificates of merit and appreciation as well as resolutions and proclamations. These provided him with the perfect medium for producing those examples of monumental printing at which he was already so adept. Pleasant contrasts to the cold grandeur of these works are the following books which Nash designed and printed:

The Lights Go Out, Juliet James' *Palaces and Courts at the Exposition*, and John D. Berry's *The City of Domes*.

The Exposition caused indirectly the formation of an organization which proved to be a good customer of Blair-Murdock and, subsequently, of Nash himself. Shortly after having learned in 1912 that the Exposition was to be held in San Francisco, E. R. Taylor, the father of the Taylor brothers; the executive W. R. K. Young; the bookman James D. Blake; and Nash approached Charles C. Moore, the President of the Exposition, with the idea of including among the Exposition's displays an exhibit of fine printing. A collector of books himself, Moore was interested. He offered the sound advice that such an idea would carry more weight if the authorities who had to approve all exhibits were petitioned by a formal committee rather than an informal group. Such a committee was formed, and it became the nucleus of the Book Club of California. The exhibit of fine printing did not materialize, but the Book Club of California, established late in 1912, became a permanent part of San Francisco's cultural life.

Although a founder of the Book Club of California, Nash was not one of its first officers. He probably could have been if he had so desired. Some of his staunchest admirers were on the Board. Nash was content with the assurance of receiving a generous allotment of the Club's printing. From 1912 to 1915, he was, of course, still with Taylor, Nash & Taylor, which printed the Club's first publications. Of the orders for Club printing which followed Nash to Blair-Murdock, one is particularly handsome. It is an edition of three Bret Harte stories: *The Luck of Roaring Camp*, *The Outcasts of Poker Flat*, and *Tennessee's Partner*.

Nash's last work for Blair-Murdock was probably this Harte book which was completed in January, 1916. That same month Blair-Murdock ceased to exist. Blair had overexpanded the firm which was in real financial difficulty by late 1915. At the same time, he had become deeply and illegally involved in recruiting men for the British armed forces. Legal action was brought against Blair and he was fined $1,000, having been found guilty of violation of section thirty-seven of the U. S. Criminal Code.[53] In February, 1916, he fled to Canada.

Nash found himself without an employer. It was probably just as well. He was a man who had grown weary of working for other men. They, in turn, had found his requirements burdensome and expensive. Nash had exhausted the possibilities of collaboration between his aspirations and the requirements of the commercial houses for which he worked. Neither Nash nor the remaining San Francisco firms which might have hired him seemed anxious to repeat the experience. Accordingly, Nash made the most important decision of his career—to become his own master and to end, at the age of forty-five, what he called his probationary period.

CHAPTER III

FIRST YEARS: 1916–1919

> San Francisco enjoys the distinction of being a paradox
> in her social and business methods. Her people are the
> most lavish in hospitality, the most generous in charity,
> the most eager for outward display, and yet the most
> susceptible to calumny against competitors, and have the
> most astonishing disregard to the credit that comes from
> keeping promises inviolably.[1]

IF JOHN HENRY NASH had read this appraisal, when it first appeared,
he would have had good cause to recall its unflattering evaluation of
San Francisco's business community when he opened his own shop
seven years later. At best, his efforts were met with indifference or
scepticism; generally they were treated with open hostility. The
reasons for this unfavorable reception are to be found, in part, in
Nash's alleged goal: to operate a press devoted solely to the production of fine printing. Additionally, Nash had already made enemies
of important members of San Francisco's book-producing community, several of whom were quick to attempt to undermine his pre-
carious position. Furthermore, he was a poor business risk, and this
fact was generally known. His capital was ridiculously inadequate,
and he had very little equipment. Finally, he could not have picked
a time when the public was less receptive to the idea of the finely
printed book, for World War I, which had halted the fine printing
movement in Europe, had already discouraged a similar movement
in this country. The rumor was widely circulated—and encouraged
in certain quarters—that Nash would be ruined within three months.[2]

Nash admits that at the time he was decidedly anxious. He had reason to be. His capital, which did not exceed $600, was nearly ex-
hausted in establishing his credit with local supply houses. The pro-
prietors of these firms had so little confidence in Nash's situation that
they did not even bother to deliver the supplies he had ordered from
them. He was forced to pick up these materials himself. His equipment was limited to bare essentials, consisting of a desk, typecases, a
composing stone, a proof planer, and necessary tools. His stock of
type was meager, including only Caslon and Cloister Old Style and

some American Old Style. His paper stock, in addition to scraps picked up at random, included Fabriano, Kelmscott, San Marco, and a few more standard lines. His quarters were a narrow room on the third floor of the Carmen-Johnson Building at 340 Sansome Street. His staff, at first, numbered only himself, a feat made possible by the fact that he farmed out most of his presswork. Nash's capital assets were obviously far from impressive.

But Nash had other and perhaps more important assets: reputation, influential friends, and the existence of an incipient market for his kind of product. Although his firm was new, Nash's reputation was well established nationally and, of more importance at this time, locally. Where expertly executed fine printing was required, no one in San Francisco could present better credentials than he to provide it. The basis of his national reputation was the enthusiastic reception his work had received in the columns of such leading trade periodicals as the *Inland Printer*, the *American Printer*, and the *Printing Art*. While this work had been done by Nash as an employee, he was able to identify it as his own. Occasionally, the firm was not mentioned at all.[3] Furthermore, Nash's liberal use of colophons in his books provided him with a most effective medium of self-advertisement. Locally, the *Pacific Printer and Publisher* had long extended to Nash's work frequent and favorable notice. Nash reached beyond the special audience to which these periodicals were primarily addressed by compiling a private mailing list of persons, with varied occupations but a common interest in printing, to whom he sent specimens of items printed by him for such firms as the Tomoyé Press, Taylor, Nash & Taylor, and Blair-Murdock. Christmas, in particular, became the annual occasion for Nash to present examples of his work to these persons. The recipients varied from conspicuous bibliophiles to businessmen with no particular bibliographic instincts.

Nash's friends in high places were in an advantageous position to proselytize for him, and this they did gladly, for they were as convinced as Nash that his work was contributing substantially to the greater glory of fine printing and of San Francisco. Persons like W. R. K. Young of the C. & H. Sugar Company and Morgan A. Gunst of M. A. Gunst & Company could guarantee for Nash all or a substantial part of the printing needed for their firms' advertising. Young, Gunst, and others at various times served as Nash's advocates on the board of the Book Club of California. Albert Bender, who had a wide circle of friends and acquaintances and a singular talent as a salesman, was an effective and generous promoter of the product Nash was trying to sell.

The interest of such persons resulted in enough orders to keep Nash in business, but these orders were generally not for the kind of work which Nash required to express at its best his particular style of printing. That style required book orders. The fine printer without substantial book orders or patronage must rely upon job printing for his chief source of income. A real dilemma results. If his orders for job printing are light, he cannot afford to produce books unless their cost has been underwritten. On the other hand, if he has a good business in job printing, he has little opportunity to work on books. Through the patronage of one man Nash was able to avoid this predicament shortly after he opened his shop.

Charles W. Clark, the elder son of Senator William Andrews Clark, Sr., belonged to the dynasty of conspicuous consumers who contributed so much to the glitter of California's reputation during the first quarter of the twentieth century. Wealthy, educated, and informed, Clark was a competent book collector. His approach to book collecting was less encompassing than that of several of his contemporaries; it was also much more scholarly and discriminating. He knew at least the rudiments of descriptive bibliography and had a good eye for the book bargain. He also chose his agents well. His collection of incunabula and the English classics was to become outstanding during the 1920's when he fell under the influence of that incomparable salesman, Dr. A. S. W. Rosenbach. It was already substantial by 1914 when, deciding to display his treasures and at the suggestion of John Howell, Clark commissioned Taylor, Nash & Taylor to print the first volume of a projected multi-volume catalogue of his library. The order was turned over to Nash's Fine Work Department. Clark was impressed with the completed volume.

Upon hearing two years later that Nash had established his own firm, Clark recalled his satisfaction with the printer's earlier work on this catalogue. Additionally, Clark was sufficiently impressed with Nash's work generally to be willing to support the new shop. Inviting Nash to call upon him at his rooms in the St. Francis Hotel, Clark explained that he wanted Nash to print the second volume of his catalogue. The commission itself was, of course, most welcome. Then Clark wrote Nash a large check on account, although the edition was to be limited to thirty-five copies, explaining that the manuscript of the catalogue would follow shortly.[4] Actually, it was not nearly ready for the press. This was Clark's generous way of encouraging Nash. Clark's gesture had inaugurated in a modest way the tradition of patronage that was eventually to set Nash's career apart from the mainstream of American printing. Whether he knew it or not, Nash had achieved success at that moment.

However, Clark's support did not itself provide sufficient income or book work, and Nash continued to cultivate other sources. He had already identified these sources during his days with Taylor, Nash & Taylor and Blair-Murdock. Among them were the local booksellers who occasionally acted as publishers. A. M. Robertson, one of San Francisco's successful booksellers, had commissioned the printing of six books from Nash's Fine Work Department at Taylor, Nash & Taylor. John Newbegin, a good friend of Nash, ordered two books from Taylor, Nash & Taylor and four from Blair-Murdock during Nash's tenure with these firms. John Howell was an occasional customer, as were such other booksellers as the California Book Company and the San Francisco Stationery Company. In the Book Club of California, Nash saw a substantial potential customer. But as important as these organizations were, private clients had provided Nash with the largest number of book commissions when he worked for Taylor, Nash & Taylor and Blair-Murdock. Fifteen books produced by Nash for these firms were printed for private clients. This number was to be increased during Nash's early independent years. Finally, special events, such as the Panama-Pacific International Exposition, occasioned substantial orders, and Nash would always keep himself well informed about such events and the printing which they required.

An analysis of Nash imprints from 1916 to 1919 reveals a pattern of an annual increase in book work as compared to an annual decrease in job and ephemera printing. Except for those spectacular

items produced "for the joy of doing," Nash preferred book printing. It alone provided him with the significant subject and sufficient
challenge he required to do his best work.

Including the Clark catalogue, Nash printed nine books in 1916.
The customers who ordered six of these books were private in-
dividuals. In addition to Clark they were Howard Shafter (*Gallant
Boys in Blue*); the Historical Landmarks Committee of the Native
Sons of the Golden West (*The Locality of the Broderick-Terry
Duel of Sept. 13, 1859*); the Seamen's Church Institute of San
Francisco (a descriptive brochure); G. E. de Vries of the Netherlands Art Exhibition (a catalogue of the circuit exhibition which
followed the Panama-Pacific International Exposition); and the
Panama-Pacific International Exposition Company (*The Legacy of
the Exposition*), a collection of comments about the exhibition by
over seven hundred visitors. The last work is squarely in the Nash
tradition of bookmaking. Its binding is particularly interesting for,
Nash proudly proclaimed in the *Announcement* for the book, "the
paper is sewed to tapes, after the bookbinding art of four centuries
ago." The book was given a prominent review in the *Inland Printer*.[5]
Its appearance under Nash's imprint was also something of a coup,
for the competition to secure its printing had been keen.

Nash was also successful in obtaining the printing of the second
of the Book Club of California's publications. This work is a deluxe
edition of Edwin Markham's popular poem *The Man with the Hoe*.
Preceded by elaborate announcements, the book was distributed
free to club members. Enclosed with it were reproductions of two
letters from Markham to Albert Bender and a photograph by Ga-
briel Moulin of the painting itself. One of Markham's letters contained praise for the printer: "It gratifies me to know that your
printer friend, Mr. John Henry Nash, is planning to print 300 copies
of this poem. I know of his remarkable work; he will give my lines
an added beauty."[6] Nash's copy of the book contains Markham's
inscription: "My congratulations: you have enfolded the Hoe-man
in a glory of print, a raiment of kings!"

However, Nash's pièce de résistance for 1916 was his own publication of T. J. Cobden-Sanderson's *The Ideal Book*. In selecting
this work on which to expend his best effort, Nash sought two ends:

to give public endorsement to the British master's ideas on the book beautiful and to set for himself the most spectacular challenge he could devise, by producing for the inspection of one of the world's leading fine printers his own version of the ideal book. Using a typical Nash maneuver, he let others do the preliminary negotiations. W. R. K. Young was selected to write to Cobden-Sanderson for permission for Nash to print an edition of *The Ideal Book.* Young's letter to Cobden-Sanderson, dated 7 June, 1914, was punctually answered and its request graciously granted.

Nearly two years passed before Nash completed his printing in an edition of 165 copies. Using Cloister Old Style type on Kelmscott paper, Nash devised a typographical design of unusual restraint. It is as if he had fallen temporarily under the spell of the tradition to which the Doves Press belongs. Perhaps for this reason Cobden-Sanderson was particularly delighted with this printing of his essay on the ideal book. Nash's audacious gamble had paid off. He now had the endorsement of one of the greatest printers of the time. Cobden-Sanderson's letter contains praise of which Nash might well be proud. Needless to say, the letter was reprinted and distributed widely. It states, in part:

What a perfectly beautiful book you have made of THE BOOK BEAUTIFUL! I am enchanted with it! Paper, type, arrangement, all combined under your clever hands to a whole which is at once a "thing of beauty" and a symbol of that great order touched with delight which I am never tired of finding to be the supreme characteristic of the universe itself![7]

Comments from other persons were equally laudatory. The usually restrained Henry L. Bullen could only express his feelings by paraphrasing the prophetic statement of the English philosopher, George Berkeley. Bullen's version said:

Westward the course of fine typography takes its way, . . . Time's noblest offspring is the last. Originally this was written in 1700 [*sic*], with reference to the planting of arts and learning in America, and the prophecy has been fulfilled. Now it may refer to East and West in America, for San Francisco has printers of great eminence of whom California may well be proud.[8]

The poet George Sterling was more specific in his praise: "It should be a matter of great pride for all Westerners that work so exquisite can be done (if only by one man) here in California."[9]

In comparison to his frequently spectacular book work, Nash's job printing seems relatively insignificant. Yet, during the first crucial years, it helped Nash to support his uncertain financial state. Varying in format from cards to broadsides and in subject from menus to school catalogues, it represents Nash at his typographical best and worst. The worst was the result of Nash's occasional impropriety—his inability to suit subject matter to treatment. The Nash style, when applied to such items as the Ames Harris Neville Company's *Discount Sheet* or the L. D. McLean Company's announcement that it was now a purveyor of Jackson's Napa Soda Water, becomes ludicrous. He was on safer ground when producing Christmas cards, for his flair here found a more appropriate medium.

The list of clients for job printing contains familiar names including, among others, the C. & H. Sugar Company, the Panama-Pacific International Exposition, the Zellerbach Paper Company, the Concordia and Bohemian Clubs, Miss Ransom and Miss Bridges' School, Hill Tolerton Galleries, and A. Schilling and Company. Their presence on that list suggests the effectiveness of Nash's salesmanship. Nash may indeed have been a less than perfect conventional businessman, but he was proving to be a superior salesman.

The pattern of Nash's business during the year 1916 was to continue, with only few modifications, for the remainder of his long career. A typical year's production included books, for booksellers, private clients, and organizations; a variety of job printing; and Nash's famous gift printings.

During the years 1917 through 1919 job printing remained an important source of Nash's income, for although the number of items decreased, his prices must certainly have increased. Local booksellers in the role of publishers continued to give Nash little support. Indeed, for this three-year period no book orders came from them at all. If Nash had expected substantial aid from that quarter, he was sorely disappointed. Private clients continued to be his best book customers. Volumes three, four, and five of the Charles W. Clark catalogue, printed, respectively, in 1917, 1918, and 1919, provided Nash with a welcome source of guaranteed income. Book and pamphlet orders from all private clients amounted to about thirty items. Familiar names appear in the imprints: Hill Tolerton Galleries, Mr. and Mrs. Charles C. Moore (*Keep the Light of Memory Burning, 1915–1918*, published to commemorate the third anniversary of the opening of the Panama-Pacific International Exposition), Thomas Nast Fairbanks of the Japan Paper Company (an attractive reprint, distributed in 1918 as a Christmas book, of William M. Thackeray's *The Chest of Cigars*), John A. Rossier, and Sara Bard Field. New names also occur, among which are to be found future substantial clients. For example, the order of the Roman Catholic Archbishop of the Diocese of San Francisco, the Most Reverend Edward J. Hanna, whose 1918 *Address* was one of Nash's first works bound in full vellum, inaugurated a tradition of patronage of Nash by Roman Catholic institutions and individuals. Ted Shawn, the famous dancer and an early Nash Christmas card client, was responsible for an order in 1918 for three thousand copies of the attractive Denishawn School catalogue.

The Book Club of California, whose membership had grown appreciably during these years, expanded its publication program with this increase. Nash continued to be selected as the printer for much of its work. In addition to the announcements and invitations which it commissioned from Nash, the Club also gave him book and pamphlet orders. While Joseph Addison's *The Vision of Mirzah* and Ina Coolbrith's *California*, which Nash printed in 1917 and 1918, respectively, were not particularly popular, his 1919 printing of *The Kasidah of Haji Abdu El-Yezdi* was.[10] The Club was especially proud of this title and indulged itself in the publication of some self-praise, which Nash also printed. It is a copy of Cobden-Sanderson's letter of commendation of the work, addressed to W. R. K. Young, at that time the President of the Club. The letter describes the book as being beautifully printed and built.

Nash received some excellent promotion during this period at no cost to himself. For example, his printing of the broadside announcement of the opening of the California Theatre in 1917 was reproduced in a full-page spread in five of San Francisco's leading newspapers—the *Bulletin*, the *Call*, the *Chronicle*, the *Daily News*, and the *Examiner*.[11] His elaborate printing of an invitation to President Woodrow Wilson from the San Francisco Advertising Club to attend the 1918 world meeting of advertisers in San Francisco was itself an important job order. The President's reply, which contained this reference to Nash's work—"May I not add just a line to say what a singularly beautiful piece of printer's work the invitation is"[12]—was, of course, widely discussed among printers and advertisers.

Nash's gift printings continued to be the talk of the trade and an increasing number of appreciative bibliophiles. One wonders whether Nash could easily afford the cost of his elaborately printed edition of the *Sermon on the Mount*, which by his own account amounted to $2,100,[13] or of Richard Hovey's *Barney McGee*. However, both received flattering and even enthusiastic comments.[14] In discussing the *Sermon on the Mount*, the *Pacific Printer and Publisher* was actually moved to describe Nash's firm as an "art-shop,"[15] although it was still sufficiently uncertain about the term to place it in quotation marks. W. Irving Way, the noted Chicago bookman, said of the same work that "in the quality of the paper, color of ink, uniformity of press work, register, and modest rubrication your work seems to me to be on a level with the best tradition of the art."[16] In the opinion of the *Pacific Printer and Publisher, Barney McGee* was an event in the printing craft on the Pacific Coast.[17] Other Nash gift items received equally high praise. Of Witter Bynner's *A Canticle of Praise*, printed by Nash in 1918 "for the Joy of the Making," according to the colophon, the *San Francisco Chronicle* judged that it was "the printer as artist adding a typographical poem to the canticle."[18] In evaluating the same work, Henry L. Bullen used the word "beautiful."[19] In praising Bynner's *The New World*, Nash's gift book for 1919, the *Inland Printer* designated Nash as one of the foremost American typographers.[20]

By the close of the year 1919, a short three and one half years after opening his shop, Nash had achieved notable reputation as a fine printer. His financial success was comparatively moderate, but it was sufficient to encourage him to continue along the same path. The fact that he was still in business at all was perhaps his greatest achievement, for he had begun his career as an independent printer with severely limited capital assets and in the face of hostility and scepticism from a large segment of San Francisco's book-producing community. His success over these formidable obstacles was, of course, based in large measure upon the quality of his work. Equally important was the efficacy of his salesmanship. The two had secured for him the active support not only of the small but enthusiastic group of San Francisco's bibliophiles, but also of other and previously undeveloped sources, including businessmen and firms and wealthy patrons of the arts who had not previously regarded printing as an art. Dominating all of these developments was the Nash mystique which by 1919 had already transformed Nash into a champion "for all that is true art and beauty in the world of typography."[21] In the view of his admirers, Nash was not to relinquish this title for many years.

Chapter IV

THE TWENTIES: SUCCESS

IF EVER a fine printer was in the right place at the right time, that man was John Henry Nash in San Francisco in the 1920's. Perhaps, among printers, only Giambattista Bodoni before him had enjoyed so perfect a combination of time and place. The Twenties in the United States, following the recovery from the jarring recession of 1920–1921, witnessed an unprecedented prosperity which was generally shared and generously expended. California, with its tradition established during the Gold Rush days of conspicuous consumption, did more than its share of the spending. Within California, San Francisco was the city most closely identified with this tradition to which it added another—the generous support of all of the arts. As an age of extravagance ruled by the cult of the salesman, the Twenties provided Nash, the expansive printer and consummate salesman, with a perfect setting for his product and his promotional method.

The Twenties also witnessed a marked increase in the number and the zeal of book collectors who vied with each other to buy copies of limited editions, finely printed books, and rare imprints. Not only ready money in the hands of many persons but also a greater awareness on their part of the pleasure, prestige, and profit to be gained from the collecting of books caused this increase. The audience for the book beautiful was no more enthusiastic at this time than in California where, as Nash said, almost a craze for fine printing existed.[1] San Francisco experienced this craze in its most virulent form. It was a fine printer's paradise.

While this paradise numbered among its elect the Grabhorn brothers, the Johnson brothers, John B. Kennedy of Kennedy-ten Bosch, Haywood H. Hunt, and others, its leading citizen was John Henry Nash. The Twenties in San Francisco were all his.

Nash's preeminence among San Francisco's fine printers during this period was based in part upon his seniority, for his reputation had been established in the preceding decades and rested upon a firm foundation. Additionally, most of his fellow fine printers were his juniors in age. However, Nash's seniority was not solely chronological. He was a peerless salesman and technician. These two roles combined to produce the Nash style which assumed, during the uninhibited Twenties, those heroic proportions which were the source of admiration for many, if also of annoyance for a few. Nash's colleagues tried to emulate his financial and critical success. None presumed to imitate his style for, as they correctly surmised, it was inimitable. Indeed, not only the style but also the entire career of John Henry Nash are probably unique in the annals of printing history.

That Nash's uniqueness was a significant cause of his remarkable success as a printer is no more apparent than during the Twenties when his success was most pronounced. In order to identify and to analyze the elements of this uniqueness which, of course, were present during all of Nash's career but which were particularly well defined at this time, this chapter consists of a topical presentation rather than a chronological one. Nash's uniqueness is composed of three elements: his printing, his patronage, and his promotion. These are discussed under the following rubrics and in the following order: "The Printing Shop" and "Printer Ordinary" describe Nash's printing. "Printer Extraordinary" considers the subject of patronage. Finally, "The Library" and "Gifts" treat promotion.

The Printing Shop

For twenty-two years the books, pamphlets, broadsides, and material in other format issued from the shop of John Henry Nash were judged by his contemporaries to be technically perfect in their composition, presswork, and binding. While Nash's artistry is under general criticism today, his technical achievement is still accorded high praise. That praise belongs first of all to Nash, but there were other persons and firms whose work for him contributed significantly to his reputation. The world-famous Nash shop was in reality an atelier, and the work bearing the master's signature was the product of many hands and many talents.

Nash's shop was primarily a composing room, although some stitching and binding were also done there. Nash's personal prejudice in favor of composition was based upon his education and his experience. He had been trained as a compositor, and when he had invested in printing equipment and a staff of pressmen he had experienced financial reverses. Thus, when he opened his own shop in 1916, he adopted the historical divison between composition and presswork.

By effecting this policy he was able to keep the size of his establishment limited both in personnel and in equipment. Never more than half a dozen people were on his regular payroll at one time, and the size of his shop, even when it was located in its commodious quarters in the John Henry Nash Building from 1925 to 1938, was modest. Its appearance was also unprepossessing.

The printing shop had little furniture and no elaborate accessories; it seemed almost spartan. The composing stone which dominated the scene was encircled by row upon row of typecases lining the walls of the shop. In the contents of these cases, however, the prevailing theme of modesty was abandoned, for by the mid-Twenties, Nash's plant had, for its size, a collection of foundry type probably unequalled both in its quantity and variety. When Nash's shop was closed in 1938, its equipment and type weighed seven tons.[2]

Nash's collection of type far exceeded any practical needs. When Nash closed his San Francisco shop in 1938 some of the type had never been used, and the remainder was still in nearly perfect condition because his editions were small in number and because his type was so plentiful. The impetus for this collection was threefold: Nash's interest in the history of printing, his archival instincts, and the evocative nature of his typography. His favorite type consisted almost entirely of modern adaptations or models of types designed in the past. Among type designers Nicolas Jenson was his ideal, and Nash was an early and constant advocate of Cloister Light Face, the cutting by ATF modelled on Jenson's elegant roman. This same high regard for Jenson caused Nash to champion, as well, another twentieth-century version of Jenson's roman—Bruce Rogers' Centaur type. Other American-manufactured types which Nash used and helped to make popular were Bodoni, Bodoni Book, Bulmer, Caslon 471, Cheltenham, Cloister Old Style, Elzevir, and Garamond. Dating from the time of his first trip to Europe in 1921, he became an inveterate buyer of European types as well, often paying handsomely for them. For 1,000 pounds of Inkunabula, for example, he spent $3,500.[3] He also assembled from purchases made during his European visits probably the greatest collection in this country of exotic typographic borders, ornaments, and initials. These items were displayed more than they were used, and Nash probably regarded them as more a part of his Typographical Library and Museum than of his printing shop. He delighted particularly in showing this collection to the younger printers among his visitors—men who had only worked with the more standard job fonts.

To play upon this incomparable instrument, excellent compositors were hired by Nash. Aside from Joseph FauntLeRoy, Nash's Superintendent, and Mrs. Fritzie Buchignani, who entered his office as an apprentice in 1923 and remained as a compositor until 1932,[4] the other compositors came and went. FauntLeRoy, who joined Nash in the fall of 1918 and who was to remain as a compositor until the spring of 1933,[5] was one of San Francisco's most competent technicians in the trade of printing. His standards were as high as those of Nash. His perseverance and patience in attaining and maintaining these standards probably exceeded Nash's, and for this reason he was much the better supervisor. His profound knowledge of the technical aspects of composition, presswork, and binding, his gentlemanly disposition, his serenity, and his sympathy with Nash's goals made him a perfect chief assistant.[6] Indeed, after having decided on the format of a book and after having set its title page, dedication, colophon, and a sample subtitle and running head, Nash turned all further responsibility for composition and presswork over to FauntLeRoy.[7] By being able to do so, Nash was free to make those public performances and private contacts that were so essential to his success. If FauntLeRoy had chosen to open his own shop, he would have been an equal to the best. That he elected, rather, to remain with Nash contributed in no small measure to Nash's own success.

Next to FauntLeRoy, Nash's most valuable employee was Mae Hartmann. Hired by Nash soon after he opened his shop, she was one of his first employees. She remained with Nash until his San Francisco shop closed in 1938. Primarily a compositor, Miss Hartmann was also called upon to keep the books, to proofread, and to assist in what binding was done at the shop. Miss Nell O'Day, appointed Nash's Librarian in 1925, sometimes stepped across the hall that separated the shop from the library to assist with proofreading and bookkeeping.

Nash's compositors served him well. Their scrupulous attention to the spacing of type—in particular their ability to avoid the white spots in a printed page which Nash abhorred—enabled Nash to present perfectly in his printing his concept of the "typographical picture." Individual works, for example his *Songs of the Singer David* (1929), exhibit a spacing that is uncomfortably tight. Generally, however, Nash's composition has been praised for the even tone of spacing.[8]

For the remaining services essential to the construction of his creations—presswork, binding, illustrations, and writing—Nash turned primarily to other talented San Franciscans. Nash's pressmen formed a crucial segment of his atelier, for flawless presswork was essential to the success of his style of printing. Because Nash declined to have any direct part in the actual printing of his material, he had from the time of the establishment of his own shop hired other firms to do this work. Among the firms and persons producing Nash's printing were the Independent Pressroom, the Trade Pressroom, Arthur Fay, John J. Neblett, Thomas Beatty and Lawton Kennedy, and Arthur Maehl.[9] Neblett and Maehl did the lion's share of this printing.[10]

As good as Nash's printers were, they would probably not have performed so well if FauntLeRoy had not been present during the printing. It was FauntLeRoy's habit, or, more likely, Nash's directive, that FauntLeRoy personally would accompany the forms from Nash's composing room to the quarters of the press and supervise every step in their printing. FauntLeRoy was a perfectionist. On one job, literally hundreds of makeready sheets might be rejected before he was satisfied.[11] He would stop the press repeatedly whenever the job was particularly difficult. For a more typical order it was still his habit to stop the press at every twentieth or thirtieth impression.[12] His relentless scrutiny allowed few imperfections to pass unnoticed. It is said of FauntLeRoy that he could see a nick in a six-point period.[13]

For most of Nash's printing a hand-fed cylinder press was used. It measured either between 25 and 38 inches or 28 and 42 inches.[14] Nash preferred a cylinder press to a platen press for most of his work because the former could guarantee more uniform impression and could allow for more accurate register. He also printed dry instead of wet in his quest for that same uniformity, since it is more difficult with wet sheet printing to obtain perfect backup. Because it was necessary to apply extreme pressure in printing on the heavy and rough paper which Nash often used, and because Nash insisted upon the paper being printed *into* rather than *through*, the pressman would often insert a sheet of thin tempered steel directly under the tympan sheet.[15] Extreme care in makeready was exercised. Haywood H. Hunt observes that he has seen Nash's pressmen cut out the dots over whole pages of lowercase "i's" when type as large as eighteen-point was used,[16] since isolated matter tends to hit the paper harder and is even more apt to perforate the paper.

While it was something of a distinction to do Nash's presswork, since his requirements tested a man's skill to its fullest and since he was willing to pay more for exceptional effort, the rewards were well earned. For one thing, Nash demanded priority attention for all of his work, and one press in the Trade Pressroom was kept at his disposal at all times under this stipulation. Additionally, he would tolerate no complaints about his requirements, and apparently none got any further than FauntLeRoy, whose standard rejoinder "You can take that up with Mr. Nash" was sufficient warning.[17]

While demanding perfect presswork, Nash presented at the same time inordinately difficult paper on which to print. Handmade and mouldmade rag paper was increasingly used by Nash for every category of his printing. During the Twenties, when he made several trips to Europe, he scoured the paper mills there for the unusual and interesting. Before this time, he had found in the Japan Paper Company a reliable supplier. Once he had visited the Van Gelder Paper Company in the Netherlands, however, he chose it as his major paper supplier. Established in 1783, this organization was by the 1920's a very large enterprise. It was the firm's quality rather than its size, however, which impressed Nash. He claimed to have placed the largest single order—two thousand reams—for handmade rag paper which the company had ever received.[18] Compared to much of the paper Nash obtained, this paper was easily handled by the pressman. The other paper was often deckled on all four edges and of a rough texture. Some of it contained fibers which could shatter the type. "If there is any paper anywhere in the world that is hard to print on," one printer is reported to have said, "John Henry Nash will find it."[19]

Nash's preference for the hand-fed cylinder press compounded the problem, for it is not equipped with an automatic side guide. Because heavy deckle is liable to drag against the stationary guide with which the cylinder press is equipped, a situation that can result in the buckling and tearing of the sheets, the pressman was forced to feed the sheets at an angle, adding to his already difficult predicament. Even the climate contributed to the tribulations of Nash's pressmen. San Francisco's variable humidity may cause expanded paper which can throw off the careful registration Nash required. Periodically, presswork had to be suspended until the weather was better. At all times, however, these problems were resolved in the name of perfection.

FauntLeRoy's responsibility ended when the printed sheets were ready for binding. While Nash's more spectacular binding was done in Europe by the Leipzig firm of Hübel und Denck, the bulk of it was executed locally; generally the workmanship was excellent. Nash's own staff was qualified to fold and to hand sew paper-covered booklets, and some tipping was also done in his shop. More ambitious binding was usually turned over to local firms, and from John Kitchen, Jr., Timothy O'Leary, and Anthony Cardoza, Nash received competent work.

Nash's requirements from his illustrators were as exacting as those from his compositors, pressmen, and binders. Because he regarded his printing as typographical pictures, he generally considered conventional illustrations to be redundant. When illustrative matter was required, Nash's aim was to make it as unobtrusive as possible. Nash's ideal illustration in his ideal book must meet these requirements: "[it] must be consistent with the volume in every aspect, sustain the same line quality as the type, have the same strength or delicacy as the paper and make-up and be expressive of the subject."[20] The typical illustrator would find these requirements to be intolerable. Nash, who was seldom tolerant of the typical, hired his own illustrators specifically to produce the kind of illustration he wanted.

The nature of the "hiring" of his first illustrators is not clear. They were probably paid by the job, and they probably worked independently of any formal association with Nash. These men included Ray F. Coyle (see as examples of his work for Nash, Eduard Eichenberg's *What the Birds Did at Hazel's Orchard*, 1916; *Sermon on the Mount*, 1917; Richard Hovey's *Barney McGee*, 1917; Witter Bynner's *The New World*, 1919; and the 1920 edition of three short stories by Ambrose Bierce); Dan Sweeney (see Joseph Addison's *Vision of Mirzah*, 1916; Ina Coolbrith's *California*, 1918; and Sir Richard Burton's translation *Kasidah*, 1919); Lawrence B. Haste (see Witter Bynner's *Canticle of Praise*, 1917); and William Rauschnabel (see *Vintage Festival*, 1920). In 1923, William H. Wilke did his first work for Nash—the frontispiece for William Andrews Clark, Jr.'s edition of Edgar Allan Poe's *Tamerlane*. Wilke was the most successful of Nash's illustrators in achieving in his work the style that Nash desired, and, following the tragic death of Coyle in 1924, he became Nash's only illustrator for several years. The association was strengthened when Wilke moved his shop from Shreve's to quarters in Nash's own shop. Between that date and the time of his withdrawal from Nash's shop during the Depression, Wilke devised for Nash frontispieces, borders, headpieces, and tailpieces for two dozen or so books and for numerous items of ephemera. A native of San Francisco, Wilke obtained his early education in art at the Mark Hopkins Art School in that city. Following further study in Paris and Florence, he returned to San Francisco, where he was elected subsequently to membership in the California Society of Etchers. Wilke's talent probably exceeded Nash's demands which required more the skill of the draftsman than the creativity of the artist. Wilke must have rebelled periodically at the close confinement of his association with Nash. Whether or not his work for Nash was the best he could do artistically, it is technically superb, particularly the drypoint etchings, described by Henry L. Bullen as "a high event in bookmaking,"[21] which he executed for the Clark books. Wilke must certainly be regarded as an important, if somewhat frustrated, member of the Nash atelier.

To write his promotional material and the texts of some of the

work he published, Nash added to his part-time staff at least three
San Francisco writers. Two of these people—Walter H. Gardner
and John Eugene Hasty—were only occasional contributors. Nash's
chief writer was also one of his most effective supporters. Edward
F. O'Day, a local journalist and free-lance writer of some importance, was an influential member of San Francisco's bibliographical
community as well; he was, for example, a charter member of the
Book Club of California. His urbane and facile pen supplied the
text for many of Nash's vacation and Christmas broadsides and for
some of the Zellerbach series of Printer's Keepsakes as well as more
substantial works, such as his Introduction to Nash's printing of the
Limited Editions Club's edition of Benjamin Franklin's *Autobiography*.

The Nash atelier, drawing on talent and equipment from many
sources, sustained fully the reputation Nash had made singlehanded-
ly during his first independent years. The performance of the members of the atelier enabled Nash to claim, with some justification,
that he had achieved an unexcelled technical perfection in the production of his imprints.

PRINTER ORDINARY

While Nash's reputation during the Twenties was based in large
part upon the work he did for his chief patrons, a substantial amount
of his income continued to come from the printing of material for
less wealthy individual clients and organizations. Nash's press was
never exclusive, either in the clientele or the categories of printing
it accepted. Nash would print any order for anyone as long as the
price was right.

The income which resulted from Nash's role as printer ordinary
was about equally divided between book and job work. Among his
customers for the former were private clients, publishers, and
bibliographical societies. Of this group, private clients were the
most important. The content of several of the books Nash printed
for private clients, the elaborate style he often applied to their production, and the high commissions he charged for them have resulted in the judgment that Nash's was a vanity press. While this
term today is the source of universal deprecation, it was not so at

an earlier period. Vanity printing was a legitimate source of income for the printer, as Nash had learned during his tenure with Stanley-Taylor, Taylor, Nash & Taylor, and Blair-Murdock.

Vanity printing had provided Nash with an important portion of his income during his fledgling years from 1916 to 1919. It was to continue to do so during the Twenties. These books represent Nash at his best and his worst artistically. Given a free hand and the right incentive, Nash could produce, in this genre, tastefully done work, but too often to his own lapses in taste were added those of his clients. The results are typographical monstrosities. Nash even descended to the use of photographs in some of these books, a practice which he had generally and wisely avoided.

From 1920 through 1929, at least one book for a private client was produced by Nash annually. Nash seems to have behaved like Robin Hood in determining how much money to exact, the wealthy paying substantially more than other clients. No one got off cheaply. These books ranged from rather slight works to large tomes. Their runs varied from as little as twelve copies for an edition of Marjorie Greenwood Josselyn's *Notes on South America with Variations!* (1920) to more standard editions of 150, 200, and 250 copies for other works. An edition of 2,500 copies of a 1923 catalogue of an exhibition of contemporary French art which was held in the San Francisco Civic Auditorium was exceptionally large.

Vanity was a major impetus for bringing private clients to Nash's shop to order books, pamphlets, and smaller items. Memorial books, either of the life of the customer or his ancestors, friends, or business associates, are common among Nash's imprints. In this category, he produced several works, the most famous of which is the biography of Phoebe Apperson Hearst.

Less serious subjects occasioned the printing of several gift books and pamphlets. Nash's own policy of lavishly dispensing books and broadsides as gifts to friends and clients set an example which was imitated by several persons. Nash was eminently qualified to do such work, interesting examples of which include a deluxe edition of 200 copies of Eugene Field's poem *Little Willie* (1921), done for Louis A. Kohn of Chicago, and a series of technically superb folios, often printed in four colors, produced for Howard J. Griffith of the American Engraving and Colorplate Company of San Francisco. The series includes such impressive works as Clarkson Dye's *Eight O'clock* (1923), Robert Louis Stevenson's *Napa Wine* (1924), Samuel Taylor Coleridge's *The Rime of the Ancient Mariner* (1926), and *El Toison de Oro* (1926), the later winning for Nash a coveted Graphic Arts Leaders Prize. A Christmas pamphlet, *The Dress of Thought,* gives evidence that Nash could produce some of his best work in this genre. This publication, in the opinion of Joseph FauntLeRoy, represents the zenith of bookprinting.[22]

Authors, desirous to have their work beautifully printed or, perhaps, even anxious for an expensive means to publish their masterpieces, also employed Nash. Those with modest incomes found Nash's prices discouraging, but occasionally there were wealthy authors. One such was Edwin R. A. Seligman, Professor of Economics at Columbia University and, at the time of his encounter with Nash, an exchange professor at the University of California. When asked by Nash how much he was prepared to spend for the printing of his *Curiosities of Early Economic Literature,* Seligman made the apparently cavalier response: "Oh, use your own judgment. I suppose it will cost somewhere between five and fifty thousand."[23] The sumptuous appearance of the printed volume strongly suggests that Nash took the quip literally and that the bill must have been closer to the latter than the former figure.

Publishers were never substantial clients, but their commissions were important to Nash because they represented recognition of his ability by an important segment of the book world. Of the West Coast publishers who employed Nash during the Twenties, John Howell, the San Francisco bookman, was at first preeminent. His usual role in connection with Nash's imprints was that of a bookseller, but he did publish three of them as well. The first such work, published in 1920, was an account of the finding in San Francisco of an important manuscript of Sir Walter Scott. It is entitled *Hugh Walpole Stumbles upon Priceless Literary Treasure in a San Francisco Bookshop* and was printed in an edition of 2,500 copies. The second Nash imprint which Howell published was Ted Shawn's biography of his partner, Ruth St. Denis. The author's and printer's natural predilection for the lavish alarmed the more practical publisher, for the biography, in two volumes, was much more expensive than anyone had anticipated. Nash was not alarmed because, for one thing, he assumed that production costs would be met from the first sales of the work. Howell apparently thought otherwise, and the misunderstanding resulted in another of those feuds for which Nash had become famous. Only one more book was printed by Nash for Howell. Probably already contracted for when the disagreement occurred, it is *Stevenson's Baby Book* (1922), the record of the childhood of Robert Louis Stevenson kept by his mother. Another western bookseller-turned-publisher, for whom Nash did printing, was Ernest Dawson of Los Angeles. In 1924, Nash printed for him *Migratory Books* by W. Irving Way, a thoroughly entertaining monograph describing the provenance of some interesting literary items that ultimately found their way to Dawson's bookshop.

Eastern publishers were never very enthusiastic about Nash as a printer of their publications. Distance was one problem; their provincialism was another. They could not imagine that any printer living outside of the great eastern publishing centers could excel the work being done locally. Occasional orders from the East were the result of the residence there of individual advocates of Nash's work. Mitchell Kennerley of New York City, for example, arranged for Nash to print Dr. A. S. W. Rosenbach's *An Introduction to Herman Melville's Moby-Dick* (1924). From Chicago, which could boast of its own tradition of fine printing, came a commission from the publisher Walter M. Hill for Nash to print an edition of Alfred E. Hammill's *Sonneteering* (1921). This order was doubly prestigious, for Hammill was the President of that city's Caxton Club. An even larger feather in Nash's cap was the order from four publishers in as many cities for a deluxe edition of Elizabeth Barrett Browning's *Sonnets from the Portuguese* (1925). The publishers were Kennerley, Dawson, Hill, and A. M. Robertson of San Francisco.

The most important commission which Nash received from an eastern publisher was the printing of a deluxe edition of 380 copies of Robert Louis Stevenson's *The Silverado Squatters*. The publisher was the prestigious firm of Scribner's. If Nash could satisfy this firm that his work was marketable through its thoroughly orthodox

channels of book publishing, there was a possibility he would receive substantial support from other large publishing houses in the
East as well. He rose to the challenge. Composition, presswork, and
paper were of the best quality. For illustrations and ornamentation
he commissioned the young artist Howard Willard to make woodcut headpieces based upon photographs taken in the Napa Valley,
the setting of Stevenson's story. The cover paper, designed with a
rich pattern of grapes and leaves, expressed, Nash hoped, the lushness
of the Napa Valley. Even the errata slip rose to the occasion in
presenting a clever play on words: "Avowel! A vowel "i" replaces
a "t" in Calistoga on page 16. I can only swear it is not consonant
with my usual vigilance to allow "t" to be served so." Selling at $30
a copy, about half of which went to Nash, the work was not a great
success. Published in 1923, the small edition was still not sold out
the following year.[24] Scribner's did not extend a second invitation
to Nash, nor other eastern firms a first, and Nash's hopes of support
from large publishing houses were ended.

Bibliographic organizations continued to give Nash support. Interested in encouraging contemporary fine printers, the prestigious
Grolier Club of New York City decided in the fall of 1921 to
sponsor a Printer's Series which would consist of books printed by
selected leading American fine printers. Six printers, including Nash,
were chosen. Each was given complete freedom in design and even
some choice in the work he was to print. Nash elected to print
Maurice Hewlett's *Quattrocentisteria*, and in the production of this
work he tried to outdo himself. Excellence in Nash's mind meant
technical perfection and the use of the best and most unusual of
material. The paper he selected on which to print *Quattrocentisteria*
met this requirement, for no ordinary printer would attempt to use
it. Unusually limp as well as deckled, the paper was a pressman's
nightmare. Even under the watchful eye of Joseph FauntLeRoy,
hundreds of sheets were spoiled when fed into the press.[25] Never
one to count costs, Nash was even less concerned, in producing this
book, to maintain a budget. His efforts were not unrewarded. While
the Grolier Club had not envisioned the Printer's Series as a contest,
Nash and his advocates felt that he had more than held his own
against the Goudys, T. M. Cleland, the Gilliss Press, Carl P. Rollins,

and Bruce Rogers. More significant than Nash's self-allotted victory was the invitation itself, for the Grolier Club was the bibliographical organization preeminent in the United States.

Three thousand miles to the west, another bibliographical organization, the Book Club of California, continued to play an important role in Nash's career during the Twenties. Its contributions were not so crucial to Nash's success as they had been during his first independent years. Nor were they, relatively speaking, financially significant, for the Club's modest resources, even during the opulent Twenties, were not equal to the prices Nash usually charged. However, to continue to print for the Club, to which nearly every Bay Area bibliophile belonged, was still important to Nash, and he made the necessary financial concessions.

In response to the Club's continued support, Nash was appropriately grateful and occasionally quite generous. First of all, as has been noted, in accepting the Club's quotations on printing costs, Nash was making significant concessions. Secondly, the Club paid Nash in a method which was burdensome; that is, he was paid for the printing of a book as copies of it were sold by the Club.[26] Nash presented to Club members at least two substantial gifts: a bibliography of its publications during its first ten years and an elaborate printing, including a facsimile of the manuscript, of Bret Harte's *Dickens in Camp*.

The Club provided Nash with the opportunity to do some of his best work, including, in particular, a handsome edition of the letters of Ambrose Bierce (1922), in which *The Argonaut* claimed it could discern "a San Francisco way to print books—a way of excellence,"[27] and an attractive printing of George Sterling's poem *The Testimony of the Suns* (1927). Bierce's *An Invocation* (1928) was judged by Joseph FauntLeRoy to be one of the finest examples to come from Nash's press.[28] Nash's printing of one of the Club's most ambitious books is equally attractive. It is *Continent's End* (1925), an anthology, edited by George Sterling, of selected works of 103 contemporary California poets. The publishing of this work strained the Club's finances, and perhaps for this reason Nash was willing to accept a reduction from his original quotation of $25 a copy to $15. He had still not been paid entirely as late as 1929.[29]

During the Twenties, Nash assumed the dual role of printer-publisher of three books. Ordinarily, he eschewed the responsibilities which went with that role. On the other hand, it gave him complete freedom to choose what to print and how to print it. His financial status and his reputation were such at this time that he could easily afford the luxury and the burden of publishing.

It is an indication of Nash's esteem for Nicolas Jenson in particular and his interest in the history of printing in general that his first publication, which appeared in 1926, should be a study of that great fifteenth-century type designer and printer. To these reasons for his choice of subject may be added a third: the recent manufacture of a recutting by Morris F. Benton, the chief designer of ATF, of a typeface modelled on Jenson's roman type. Entitled Cloister Light Face, this type was first used publicly in Nash's debut publication. Written by Henry L. Bullen and entitled *Nicolas Jenson, Printer*, the work is an interesting and sound appraisal of Jenson's contributions and their influence on the subsequent development of type design. Accompanying each of the 207 copies of this edition is a leaf from Jenson's 1478 printing of Plutarch's *Vitae Parallelae Illustrum Virorum*, volume two.

Nash's design for this work attempts to evoke Jenson's style. The typography is, therefore, restrained. Bullen marvelled at the presswork and praised Nash's selection of the proper paper.[30] The type, to be used correctly, required the soft, roughly surfaced paper which had the effect, during the printing process, of thickening the lines of type. Nash showed in this first use of Cloister Light Face that it could be an effective and beautiful type. He had paid fitting tribute to Jenson in this work and in so doing he had also brought honor to himself. The reviewer for the *New York Times Book Review* praised not only this work but Nash's printing in general. In his opinion, Nash had done some of the "very finest" original and reproductive printing issued in America.[31]

Nash further asserted his interest in fine printing with the second of his publications, the handsomely printed 1929 volume on the subject of T. J. Cobden-Sanderson and the Doves Press. His interest in Cobden-Sanderson had already occasioned two editions printed by him of *The Ideal Book*. This work was more ambitious, for in addition to his third printing of *The Ideal Book*, it contained as well a bibliography of Doves Press imprints, and articles on the Doves Press and Cobden-Sanderson by A. W. Pollard, Emery Walker, and himself. Also, each copy of this edition included a leaf printed by Cobden-Sanderson.

Cobden-Sanderson's widow, whom Nash had met in Hammersmith and later in San Francisco, gave encouragement to the project as did Walker by contributing his essay gratis. Pollard required a modest fee for his essay. The Doves Press oversheets, which Nash purchased from Cobden-Sanderson's son, Richard—these included twenty sheets on vellum and 312 on paper—were probably not inexpensive, nor was the cost of Nash's own printing of this work. But high production costs were not unusual in Nash's shop in 1929.

Nash's artistic restraint in this work is unusual. *Cobden-Sanderson and the Doves Press* owes its subdued appearance, no doubt, to Nash's aim in this work of paying appropriate homage to the British master. He describes his purpose in the *Announcement* which preceded the publication of this work by several weeks:

> The effort has been in this publication to derive beauty from the utmost simplicity of treatment. Ornament of a formal sort there is none, and I concentrated on true spacing and most vigilant presswork. My aim was to make a book that would be not unworthy of the great man it was designed to honor, and I hope sincerely that I have not fallen too far short of that goal.

Nash did not fall short of perfect imitation!

Nash's most ambitious and, in the opinion of many critics, his most artistically successful publication actually predated both the Jenson and Cobden-Sanderson works in its origins, for he had begun printing at a piecemeal rate his monumental edition of Dante's *Divine Comedy* in 1923. On this one work Nash was to lavish for the next six years more attention and probably more money than on any other. Nash regarded it as his *magnum opus*, an opinion that has been generally shared.

That Nash should choose the *Divine Comedy* for this signal honor was less the result of his interest in poetry or Dante than of his friendship with Aurelia Reinhardt, the President of Mills College. While it is true that he had printed Boccaccio's *Life of Dante* as a gift book in 1923, he can hardly be described as a Dante scholar or even a Dante enthusiast. President Reinhardt *was* both, her English language translation of *De Monarchia* having been published in 1904 by Houghton-Mifflin. Additionally, her opinion carried great weight with Nash. In urging him to print the translation by Melville Best Anderson of the *Divine Comedy* she was showing her regional prejudice as well, for Nash's edition would glorify both California letters and fine printing. When she complained that she was tired of "seeing all the pretty, little books all the printers were turning out" and wished that someone would do "a monumental work that would last,"[32] Nash was completely captivated. He could not resist so great a challenge.

Having convinced Nash to undertake the printing of the *Divine Comedy*, President Reinhardt, with Nash, had next to persuade the translator to give his permission. Melville Best Anderson, the Dean of the English Department at Stanford University, could look back in 1923 on a distinguished career as a scholar and teacher which began with his appointment at that university by President David Starr Jordan. Professor Anderson had worked on his translation of the *Divine Comedy*, one of the few attempts to retain in the English language the *terza rima* form of the original, for nearly thirty years. The translation had already been published in a singularly drab edition by World Book Publishing Company in 1921. Anderson was intrigued with the prospect of it appearing in the elegant raiment which Nash would supply, as any author would have been at that time. His affirmative response to Nash's request for permission to print this translation was also enthusiastic. Furthermore, he agreed to provide an introduction, giving a historical setting to the poem. There is no indication that he received any stipend or royalty, and he does not seem to have expected one. The honor to his work of bearing the Nash imprint was sufficient reward.

The permission of World Book, which held the copyright, was also needed, and for this reason the project, for a time, seemed destined to collapse. Unlike the generous Anderson, World Book expected financial compensation. The fact that the President of that firm, Caspar W. Hodgson, was an alumnus of Stanford and a former pupil of Anderson seemed to bode well for an accommodation, and indeed Hodgson offered what would have been considered in most quarters to be a reasonable contract. But there remained the problem of Nash's decided aversion to compromise in general and to publishers in particular. His response to Hodgson's offer concluded: "I think we had better all forget the whole matter. It sounds like too much business for me to fool with." and ended with the obvious threat that "I understand that Wicksteed did a Comedy, if so I may use it."[33] Hodgson's mild rejoinder contained, in fact, further compromise on his part. "I am somewhat reconciled to your position as artist printer," he wrote, "which looks down upon the common herd of publishers who sell books." But then, he went on to say:

I admit that attitude riled me a little to start on but your book goes a long way to pulling me out of it. You know, Nash, this earth is ruled by natural laws and every man has to live by it whether artist or ditch digger. Somebody has to pay the bills even of an artist, but I like you just the same and I am going to make it possible to have you print Anderson's Dante even if I have to give it to you.[34]

In effect, he did give the rights to the printing of the *Divine Comedy* to Nash, for the final agreement stipulated only that Nash protect World Book's copyright and that he deliver ten sets of his edition to World Book and ten to Anderson.

Having acquired the permission of translator and publisher, Nash commenced the production of his masterpiece. Considerable thought went into the design of the work. It was decided that there would be four volumes—one for each of the cantos and the fourth for Anderson's Introduction. The paper, which Nash ordered from the Van Gelder paper mills in The Netherlands, bears as watermarks his name, the Van Gelder mark, and a unicorn. His type is also unique, or was so at the time, for the Cloister Light Face which he chose had only recently been issued by ATF. Also, Nash's typographical design is unusually restrained, suggesting as it does the style of Nicolas Jenson. In this work Nash relies for design on the effective interplay of the typeface, paper, composition, presswork, and binding. The last was done in full vellum by the Leipzig firm of Hübel und Denck. The only color introduced is the dull blue of the ruled margins. There is in this work an elegance which results from the "nice restraint"[35] which dominated its design.

The set was in danger of not appearing at all, for progress was at times painfully slow and always contingent upon how much time could be wrested from the shop's busy schedule. No author waited so patiently for the birth of his work as did Melville Best Anderson. An elderly man when the first pages were printed, Anderson was finally moved to ask, several years later, if it was likely that he would live to see the Dante finished.[36] Finally, in 1928, the printing had progressed to the point where Nash could see the end, and he began an elaborate advertising campaign. This was crowned with the appearance of a costly *Prospectus* which was, in itself, sufficiently attractive for booksellers to ask for extra copies.

In the *Prospectus*, Nash assumed the role of scholar-printer. More particularly, he played a twentieth century Aldus, and to perform his part more effectively he "assimilated," he said, the advice that Jean Grolier gave to his protegé in a letter that contained, in Nash's opinion, a classic statement of the printer's responsibility:

You will care with all diligence that this work, when it leaves your printing shop to pass into the hands of learned men, may be as correct as it is possible to render it. I heartily beg and beseech this of you. The book, too, should be decent and elegant; and to this will contribute the choice of the paper; the excellence of the type, which should have been but little used, and the width of the margins.

Having quoted the greatest of bibliographical advisors, Nash then went on to state to what degree he had followed this advice:

It is my sincere hope that I have met these requirements. For more than five years now I have been reverently turning the pages of the great poet, striving always to make this presentation of his masterpiece a monument alike to him, to his translator, and to the printing art. It has been an experience rich in intellectual reward.[37]

In the extravagant late Twenties, Nash found ready buyers for the *Divine Comedy* at the price of $200 a set. He was to say somewhat ruefully several years later, in the midst of the Depression, that he could as easily have charged $500.[38] Leading bookdealers, such as Dr. A. S. W. Rosenbach and Walter M. Hill, requested several sets, as did Nash's patron William Andrews Clark, Jr., who spoke for ten. Nash's faithful clients placed orders for most of the remaining copies long before the work was published, earlier solicitations, in the form of individual letters which predated the appearance of the *Prospectus*, having been quite successful. The *Prospectus* served no practical purpose; it was merely Nash's overture to the main event.

The *Divine Comedy* was hailed as a masterpiece of American bookmaking. "Never have I been so thrilled," said Nash's old colleague of Tomoyé Press days, Morgan Shepard.[39] "At last you are issuing a book that is worthy of you," wrote his friend Mitchell Kennerley.[40] Henry L. Bullen's response was warmly enthusiastic:

This Dante is a perfect work of typography, classical in design—a Cellinilike demonstration of how beautiful typography may be made without the aid of other embellishing arts. Nothing in pure typography has ever been done that surpasses your Dante. I can recall only three works in pure typography which may be compared with it. I write this after careful reflection and mental review of what has been done since Gutenberg.[41]

From Europe came the news that the King of England had selected the set for inclusion in the Royal Library at Windsor.[42] Pope Pius XI, who had been given a presentation copy, paid Nash the supreme compliment. Nash was presented with an apostolic blessing, a beautifully hand-lettered manuscript containing a finely executed miniature of the head of Dante. His Holiness wrote under his signature "grato animo"—with grateful heart.

Only one review was less than enthusiastic, and for this impertinence its author was severely and publicly chastized by the outraged Bullen. The malefactor was Carl Purington Rollins, the distinguished director of Yale University Press, and the editor, at the time of the appearance of the *Divine Comedy*, of the "Compleat Collector" section of the *Saturday Review of Literature*. He was known among Nash's allies as a member of the so-called hostile Goudy crowd,[43] and for this reason it was assumed that his appraisal of any work by Nash would be prejudiced. His review of the *Divine Comedy* in this respect did not disappoint Nash's advocates, although today it seems temperate and sensible. But at the time, anything less than enthusiastic endorsement of Nash's *magnum opus* must be, according to such persons as Bullen, the result of a perverse judgment. Rollins' review, while praising the composition, presswork, and binding, suggested some reservations about Nash's artistry. In particular, Rollins found Nash's rules somewhat objectionable: "simple as they are, they are not so simple as they should be."[44] Bullen's criticism of this somewhat enigmatic observation is well taken: "How would you make them more simple?"[45] he asked. Bullen then went on to explain, in the exasperated tone of an irate schoolmaster, why the rule scheme was so appropriate: "As the main text is poetry, each line ending irregularly, and accompanied with side notes, the rules are not simply decorative, but have the purpose of giving coherency to the pages, in a manner not otherwise possible."[46] A reviewer, he scolded, should think of these things. His concluding argument, an appraisal of Nash's significant role in the development of fine printing in America, is eloquent:

The subscribers to this great and new addition to the literature of Dante received a work as perfect as it is possible to make in the present high state of the arts of the book. John Henry Nash is America's greatest master of the typographic art. There is no position in the typographic field he could not adequately dominate . . . He has chosen to confine his activities to the highest plane of his art, in which his actual personal participation in every detail is required, and in which he has, therefore, achieved preeminent success. . . . I have had better opportunities of knowing Mr. Nash than you have had. I suppose your manifest prejudice is based on hearsay. Know then that his is a dominating personality; petty people are apt to misunderstand him; he is a sincere *lover* of his art and of all sincere folks who practice it. He has had and still has an extraordinary influence on the improvement of printing in the printing houses which day by day are doing the work required by the progressive population of the Pacific Coast, where printing is not a whit behind printing East of the Mississippi. He is highly esteemed by the numerous learned bibliophiles and collectors who have made California libraries the envy of the East. By his effort and example he has caused the art and industry of printing to be more generally respected on the Pacific Coast than anywhere else in America. No other printer in America is so influential. He is rated as a big man by the big men in other professions and industries on the Pacific Coast. Withal he is tenderhearted and sensitive, as men usually are who are frank, free-handed, and straight-forward in every relation of life. As a master printer he holds his head high for the honor of his profession. As a craftsman he is unpretentious, thoroughly democratic, even humble. A great personality, he is ever the friend of aspiring students. A hater of pretence and of unfair persons, Mr. Nash has an extraordinarily large and devoted following of wellwishers, both among the influential and among those striving upwards. This is the man you have been unfair with; yet you cannot teach him anything in the arts of the book or in the refinements of life.[47]

This "work as perfect as it is possible to make" is talked about surprisingly little today, and few copies have been sold in the intervening years, although there are, of course, few copies to be sold. Any objective critic today must certainly agree with Lawton Kennedy's appraisal: "The Dante will stand if not as a great artistic monument, then at least as one of the great monuments of American printing from its excellence of craftsmanship."[48] The publication of this work, of the Cobden-Sanderson study, and of Nash's gift work, the *Psalms of the Singer David*, made the year 1929 his *annus mirabilus*, and Nash a giant among printers.

Job printing continued to be an important part of Nash's business, although he pronounced very little about it publicly or privately. The lack of ledgers can allow one only to speculate on the prices Nash charged for job orders and the percentage of his income which came from job printing. Occasional references by Nash and others to individual commissions place a few pieces into the puzzle and suggest clearly that Nash was paid very well indeed for this type of work. Two examples can serve as illustration. Nash tells us that for printing for a millionaire, whose name he does not supply, ten thousand letterheads and six thousand envelopes, he charged $1,690.[49] He speaks elsewhere of being paid $10,000 by the San Francisco Cadillac dealer Don Lee for designing and printing one page of advertisement.[50]

Nash's job work included a wide variety of items, from stationery, labels, and business cards to commemorative broadsides, Frenchfolds, pamphlets, and his famous Christmas cards. School catalogues were also numerous, and Nash seems to have had a corner on the printing commissioned by most of the Bay Area's prestigious private educational institutions. Advertising and promotional material produced for business firms was also extensive, and included some examples of Nash's very effective typography in this medium. Most of this work was done for local organizations with the notable exception of the Japan Paper Company. Nash's printing of the *Ventura Mission*, the house organ of the United Refining Company of Los Angeles, was much talked about and won for Nash's clients in 1924 a prize of $300 offered by *Postage*, a monthly magazine devoted to direct mail advertising.[51] *Don Lee Spirit*, the house organ of San

Francisco's Don Lee Cadillac, was equally famous. Nash's association with Lee apparently resulted in his appetite for Cadillacs which gave rise to the legend that he once exchanged with Lee a bill for the printing of a Christmas card for a Cadillac. For the San Francisco Chamber of Commerce he supervised the production of *Fascinating San Francisco*, a work which appeared during the late Twenties in tens of thousands of copies.

Probably Nash's most spectacular and most widely appreciated job printing was done for the Zellerbach Paper Company, also of San Francisco. In addition to its excellent advertising organ, *The Informant*, the Zellerbach Company issued as well during the Twenties its remarkable Printer's Keepsake series which was printed by Nash. Between 1923 and 1928, handsomely printed French-folds suitable for framing appeared on Gutenberg, Garamond, Franklin, Bodoni, and Morris. For each, a page of text, giving a brief history of the printer's work, was faced with a portrait in color of the printer, reproduced from the original oil paintings in Nash's own collection. Nash's typography for this series was always evocative and carried his attempt at allusiveness as far as possible. The Morris Keepsake, for example, uses Satanic type, ATF's version of Morris' Chaucer type. The borders are reproductions of those found on two pages of Morris' projected printing of Froissart's *Chronicles*, also in Nash's possession. The Printer's Keepsake series is still avidly sought by collectors, and it continues to bring honor not only to Nash but to Zellerbach as well.

Nash was a very successful producer of job printing which continued during the Twenties to be a part of his output. While, publicly, he preferred to attribute his success to his few important patrons, it should not be forgotten that, through his job printing, he received widespread support from a large segment of the community.

PRINTER EXTRAORDINARY

Patronage transformed the unusual career of John Henry Nash into the extraordinary. No printer of his time and few before it received such generous support as did Nash during the Twenties. That patronage in itself gave credence to Nash's claim that he was an artist and, therefore, that a printer could be an artist. So did the caliber of his two chief patrons themselves, for William Andrews Clark, Jr. and William Randolph Hearst were outstanding art collectors of the time. The support which these men gave to Nash, more than any other act, set him on the royal highway of fine printing.

Hearst paid the largest sum of money for any one commission which Nash was to receive. Clark's continuing financial and spiritual support was more significant, for it made the extraordinary character of Nash's career possible.

The second son and the namesake of William Andrews Clark, Sr., the Montana copper king, Clark, Jr., had inherited wealth and position. In his own right, he was an ambitious and talented man, and his career soon proved that he could achieve eminence through his own efforts. As a businessman he was intelligent and shrewd. His development of the family mines in Montana and, later, in Arizona and his stock investments had made him conspicuously wealthy in an age of great fortunes. Unlike many of his American millionaire associates, however, he was also an educated and cultured man.

His formal education was somewhat peripatetic. His earliest years were mostly spent in France and he was to retain a prejudice for things French for the remainder of his life. His primary and secondary schools were a variety of public and private institutions in America. While his elder brother, Charles, entered Yale, he chose the University of Virginia, an institution equally capable of educating gentlemen. He was regarded as an outstanding student. Diligent and interested in his studies and deeply fond of his school, he was later to characterize his two years there as among the happiest of his life.[52] He received the degree of Bachelor of Laws in 1899, and was initiated into Phi Beta Kappa and Phi Delta Phi.

Returning to Montana the next year, he opened a law practice in Butte, but his increasingly varied interests in several enterprises caused him to abandon in a short time the restrictions of a law office. It was also about this time that he established residence in Los Angeles and commenced an annual regime that was to become a kind of royal progress between that city, Montana, where he maintained a summer lodge, the eastern United States, and Europe, in particular Paris.

By the second decade of the twentieth century, he had created a financial empire which could more or less take care of itself. He was free to devote his time and energy to his favorite cultural pursuits. These were expressed primarily through his philanthropic acts. Sometimes humanitarian,[53] more frequently cultural, they were always identified by good taste and intelligence.

An accomplished amateur violinist and an enthusiastic connoisseur of music, Clark almost single-handedly established the Los Angeles Philharmonic Orchestra in 1919. He supported it, to the tune of three million dollars, for the next fifteen years. His intelligent direction as much as his money made this organization outstanding in a short period of time.

His cultural pursuits were not limited to music. An avid reader, he made the easy step, once his interests were aroused, to book collecting. Perhaps his brother Charles cultivated his early interest in books. In any case, William soon developed his own decided tastes. These were rather catholic at first, ranging over the whole of English literature and including American and French authors as well. Always a discriminating collector he seldom bought libraries *en bloc* and soon determined to concentrate upon English literature of the seventeenth and eighteenth centuries, although he could never resist collecting at the same time such favorites as Chaucer, Shakespeare, Scott, Dickens, and Wilde. He bought deliberately and critically, choosing not to follow the rather spectacular example of massive book collecting set by his neighbor, Henry E. Huntington. Rather, Clark decided upon a policy of seeking representation, not completeness. When he died, his library was relatively small, consisting of only about 18,000 volumes, but for its size and in its areas of specialization it was outstanding.

As a book collector, Clark was a thorough man with the meticulous mind of the good lawyer that he was. He taught himself the rudiments of bibliography by examining those briefs of the book collector's world—catalogues and bibliographies. He also read widely in the history of printing. Clark had the instincts of the specialist but knew in this field that he did not have the knowledge. Aware of the snares and pitfalls awaiting the amateur in the bibliographical jungle, he consulted experts and, understanding the value of their advice, paid handsomely for it. His book dealers were among the best and most reliable, including George D. Smith and the Maggs Brothers of London and, a little later, Dr. A. S. W. Rosenbach of Philadelphia. Locally, he turned for assistance to the Pasadena bookseller George M. Millard, who is said to have first introduced him to the pleasures of collecting examples of fine printing[54] which led him initially to form his outstanding collection of Kelmscott and Doves Press imprints and subsequently to patronize Nash.

When Clark decided it was time to publish a catalogue of his collection, he turned for expert bibliographical advice in its preparation to Robert E. Cowan, the San Francisco collector, bookdealer, and the compiler of *A Bibliography of the History of California and the Pacific West, 1510–1906*, which Nash had printed for the Book Club of California in 1914. Cowan was at once an accomplished scholar and businessman, a combination which Clark particularly appreciated. "Sir Robert," as he was called by his colleagues, was also a gentleman, a status which the fastidious Clark insisted upon in his bibliographical associates.

Cowan was engaged by Clark in 1919 as his bibliographical collaborator. That same year, with the assistance of his secretary, Cora Sanders, and of Cowan, Clark prepared the first of the twenty volumes which were to comprise his library's catalogue. Dividing his extensive English literature collection into two parts, he issued in 1920 the first volumes of *Early English Literature: 1519–1700* and *Modern English Literature*. The catalogue of his collection of *The Posthumous Papers of the Pickwick Club* appeared that same year.

The printer of these elaborate and costly first volumes was John Henry Nash, and they represent his first orders from Clark. The two men apparently had not had previous dealings. It seems almost inevitable that Clark should have chosen Nash to print his catalogue, for he was surrounded by Nash's advocates and indoctrinated with the Nash mystique. Even more direct an influence was the example of Charles Clark's own library catalogue, so attractively printed by Nash. George M. Millard, who had William Clark's ear, was deeply impressed by Nash's work for Charles Clark: "I have examined the volume carefully—read it through in fact," he wrote to Nash of Volume Two. "It is my opinion that you there have reached the high-water mark of good Printing.[55] Nash had himself sent William

Clark several examples of his work. Clark was impressed and probably flattered. In turn, he paid Nash the high compliment of incorporating these Nash items into his library. The strongest advocate for Nash must certainly have been Cowan, who had a very high regard for Nash's work, including the printing of Cowan's bibliography of Californiana. Like Millard, Cowan found Nash's printing of Charles Clark's catalogue to be exceptionally good. He said, in part, in a letter of appreciation to Nash that "in this newest conception of your noble and time honored calling you have given us a volume which, in its perfect proportion of artistic beauty and finished excellence, is most gratifying and most unusual in a state and country so new as ours."[56] Cowan, then, would certainly have endorsed Nash highly as a candidate for the printing of William Clark's catalogue, and Clark, who deferred to Cowan in most things bibliographical, would have given great weight to Cowan's opinion.

That opinion proved to be well justified. Nash presented in these volumes a typographical plan completely in keeping with the quality of the collection which they record. The composition and presswork are nearly flawless. Even more impressively, the catalogue is said to be almost free of typographical errors, thanks primarily to the diligence of Joseph FauntLeRoy, who was responsible for the proofreading.[57] Nash's price for the printing of these volumes is not known; it would not have been less than that which he had charged William Clark's brother Charles. By any reckoning, the commission was a handsome one, and the printing during the following years of the remaining seventeen volumes, including the Kelmscott and Doves Press bibliographies, and of the unexeclled collection of Wilde and Wildeiana, provided Nash with an assured source of income.

Nash's appointment to print the first volumes of the catalogue began an association between William Clark and himself that was to carry Nash's career as a fine printer to new heights. At the same time, it placed Clark, in the opinion of some observers, among the elect group of patrons which included Jean Grolier and the Duke of Parma.

Clark enjoyed playing the role of patron. It gave him pleasure to be responsible for new Nash printings and to see his name on the title page of books said to be masterpieces. Catalogues, however, have their limitations of display and, besides, Clark wanted to share with fellow bibliophiles some of the individual treasures in his collection. He evolved an idea which allowed him to gratify all of his bibliophilic desires. That idea took the form of a series of annual publications which became known as his Christmas books. On them he expended that same concentration of effort which could produce a fortune, or a symphony orchestra, or such an architectural gem as his library. Like the directors of the Los Angeles Philharmonic Orchestra and the library's architect Robert D. Farquhar, Nash was given time and resources to produce that perfection which Clark demanded. Additionally, he was confronted with the kind of challenge which could evoke from him some of his best artistic and technical triumphs.

Each year Clark would select one of his favorite books and turn it over to Nash, who prepared a close facsimile of the original and his own reprinting of the text, based upon the best available edition. Specially processed paper was employed in the exacting printing from copper photoengravings of the facsimile editions. The two volumes were then bound, the Nash version elaborately, boxed, and presented by Clark during the Christmas season to a select group of friends and institutions. An edition never numbered more than 250 copies, and the first ones each comprised only 150 copies. Clark regarded these books as his private domain, closely supervising their distribution and seldom allowing Nash to use them to advertise his printing.

The first of these elaborately constructed works, a printing of *Adonais*, appeared in 1922, the centenary of Percy Bysshe Shelley's death. Clark had a particular fondness for Shelley and Keats, first of all as great poets, but also as men who, during their lifetimes, had been unjustly reviled. Clark's Introduction to the elegy is informative and effectively written. The facsimile of the 1821 Pisa edition is a masterpiece of faithful reproduction, but it is Nash's own edition of the poem which is most impressive. Subdued in style and suggestive of the dignity befitting an elegy, Nash's typographical scheme seems to be completely appropriate. The composition and presswork are nearly perfect. The frontispiece is a lovely photoengraved colored reproduction of the original crayon and watercolor portrait of Shelley executed by George Clint. William Wilke provided exquisitely devised ornamental borders. Nash turned for the printing of the frontispiece to his close San Francisco friend Howard J. Griffith, who used four colorplates to reproduce the original. Appropriately, Clark dedicated this first of his Christmas books to Nash "whose Preeminence in the Art of Typography is internationally known, whose devotion to his art should be emulated by all of the craft, whose knowledge of printing should be a source of inspiration to their renewed efforts in behalf of the typographical art, and whose finished works are unexcelled."[58]

Clark was delighted with his first Christmas book, as were its recipients, and he paid the bill of $8,000[59] without hesitation and certainly with no idea that he was probably making printing history in America. Few clients in modern times had paid to a printer so large a sum for so small an order.

The artistic and critical success of *Adonais* whetted Clark's appetite for additional Christmas books and Nash's for larger profits. This is not to suggest that Nash was exploiting Clark or that he even thought he was doing so. Rather, Clark's generosity educated Nash. In accepting the price of the Christmas books, Clark did more than anyone else to substantiate the validity of Nash's talk about the printer as artist.

Edgar Allan Poe's *Tamerlane* was Clark's 1923 Christmas book. In selecting this work, Clark was recalling his pleasant student days at the University of Virginia where, in 1897, he had helped to organize a committee of students called the Poe Memorial Association. It was the students' purpose to devise a fitting way to commemorate the fiftieth anniversary in two years' time of Poe's death. The result was a bust of Poe, executed by the sculptor George Zolany, which was unveiled on October 7, 1899, and placed in the Library of the University. In searching for the portrait of Poe to be reproduced in the frontispiece of his Christmas book, Clark returned to that bust, of which photographs were taken and from which a composite drypoint etching was made by William Wilke. Clark again provided the Introduction to the work. The facsimile volume was made from the 1827 edition, while Nash's rendition employed the text of the 1845 edition as it appeared in the *Complete Works of Edgar Allan Poe* (1902) edited by J. A. Harrison. Nash used a recutting of Garamond type which, at his urging, ATF had only recently produced.

A speech made by Nash before the San Francisco Advertising Club in 1925 contains an interesting description of Clark's reception of his second Christmas book. If Nash, in this recounting, seems to be guilty of excessive bravado, one must remember his audience and the pride which he must have felt in his accomplishments. The following passage from that speech contains enough of the truth to warrant quoting:

I remember that I only charged him $8,000 for the other book and got away with it so easy that I decided to boost up the price a little bit and finally made this bill out for $9,500. As usual, I delivered ten books to him. He took one of the books and looked through it for an hour or more, reading here and there in it. He put the book under his arm and went into the garden. Finally he said, "Did you bring the bill on this?" I thought something was wrong. I said "I am going to stay with you for a week and want to be happy while I am here so I am not going to give you the bill until I leave." He looked at it and said "I am very sorry about this. If you had made the bill $15,000 I would have been more than pleased."[60]

Nash did not need a second invitation to charge Clark's suggested prices. For *Some Letters of Oscar Wilde to Alfred Douglas, 1892–1897*, presented by Clark as his 1924 Christmas book, Nash not only selected Clark's $15,000 figure but with a flourish added $500 to it. The work, however, is a virtuoso piece of facsimile printing and required more than two years to finish. Nash was set the task of reproducing the letters on paper similar in size, color, and texture to the originals, several of which had been written on engraved and steel-die printed stationery. There were also two-color letterheads of the Café Suissé in Dieppe to contend with. Some of the letters were from eight to twelve pages long, and all were of various sizes. The facsimiles, printed from copper plates, are masterpieces of faithful reproduction. But the binding of the letters which are of various sizes and length and written on both sides of the sheets is even more impressive. Nash's ingenious Supervisor, Joseph FauntLeRoy, devised a solution for the binding of the work. Treated as separate signatures, the letters were stitched to stubs which were then pasted onto the pages. To keep the paper smooth, each stub was pressed with a hot electric iron. The method worked, and the finished volume was regarded by several authorities as a marvel for this reason alone. The frontispiece is a reproduction in photogravure from a photograph of Wilde in Clark's library. Each of the letters is also printed but this time in the same volume which contains the facsimilies. Clark asked Dr. Rosenbach to do the Preface. Everyone connected with the making of this work was delighted with the results. It remains today a fine example of facsimile printing.

For the next six years, Nash created one masterpiece of flawless bookmaking after another for Clark in the Christmas book series. For Thomas Gray's *Elegy Written in a Country Churchyard* (1925), Nash's profits from which are said to have been $17,760,[61] Caslon Old Style is used very effectively. Nash had originally preferred Fell type, but the Oxford University Press was understandably reluctant to loan its type to him and was not interested in providing further castings from the matrices. The following year, Clark selected Oliver Goldsmith's *The Deserted Village* as his Christmas book. *The Deserted Village* contains the first of several frontispieces which were etched by William Wilke from casts made of bronze plaques struck by the American sculptress Helen Hall Culber. It was Clark's practice to examine several available likenesses of the author of each of his Christmas books and then to send his final selection to Miss Culber, who resided in Rome. She would then make a bronze plaque of the portrait from which, in turn, a plaster cast was made and sent to Wilke in San Francisco. The process was time-consuming and expensive. Wilke's first attempt at the Goldsmith did not satisfy Clark,[62] but his second likeness of Goldsmith was acceptable. Clark demanded perfection and he came close enough to it, according to Henry L. Bullen, to make printing history. Bullen, who was on Clark's gift book list, noted in his letter of thanks to Clark:

It is a long time since a book of its equal in attractiveness has been published. In fact, as I pause and take a backward look, I fail to remember its equal in attractiveness . . . Morris' Chaucer [is] much more magnificent, but not nearly so attractive. [*The Deserted Village*] is much to be preferred to the best examples of the Doves and Ashendene Presses, in which severe simplicity, commendable as it is, but marks the rigidity of the printers' ideas and their lack of versatility. The book is simple; it is technically perfect; and it redeems American book typography from the accusation of being cheerless.[63]

For 1927, the Christmas book was Elizabeth Barrett Browning's *Sonnets from the Portuguese*, which is doubly interesting because the facsimile is from the Wise forgery. In 1928, Clark chose Alexander Pope's *Essay on Criticism*.

The increasingly opulent and costly Christmas books, like the decade from which they came, reached their zenith in the year 1929 with the publication of John Dryden's *All for Love*, the most expensive and lavish of the series. Nash's bill for this work was $37,000, a sum exceeded, among all of Nash's productions, only by that which he charged William Randolph Hearst for the printing of the biographies of Hearst's mother and father. But while the Hearst books were printed in editions of one thousand copies, *All for Love* consists of only 250. In choosing the Dryden play on which to lavish so much effort and money, Clark was showing his pride in his superlative Dryden collection and his special fondness for *All for Love*. This fondness had already resulted in the creation of the thirteen handsome murals depicting scenes and characters from the play, which adorned the drawing room of his library. In addition to the frontispiece portraits of Dryden and Shakespeare—the latter is included because in his Introduction Clark makes a comparative study of *All for Love* and *Antony and Cleopatra*—Clark decided to adorn his work as well with reproductions in color of these murals. This was to be the only Christmas book for which Clark set aside his and Nash's aversion to the inclusion of illustrations other than frontispieces. Color photographs were taken of the murals, then transferred to glass transparencies from which the final colorplates were made. William Wilke made a special trip to Los Angeles to sketch the murals so that the colorplate photographs could be reproduced in proper perspective. The negative plates and the paper (a special antique stock) were then sent to Germany for development and printing by a special collotype process used by the Berlin printer Bruno Deja. Nash, who had by this time turned to European sources for special paper, types, and binding, now employed a European firm as well for special printing. The results are exceptional, and the plates are among the finest reproductions of this sort ever accomplished.

In *All for Love*, Nash had created for his great patron one of the most perfectly executed books that money could buy. At the same time, with this work Nash had carried the Christmas series as far as it could advance technically and artistically. One wonders in what direction the series would have gone if the Depression, which followed in earnest upon the appearance in 1930 of the last book in the uninterrupted series, had not occurred. That work, Robert Louis Stevenson's *Father Damien*, for which Nash received $22,375, is presented in more chaste attire than Dryden's play, and its appearance seems almost anticlimactic. Posterity has not seemed to agree with Bullen that in *Father Damien* Nash had produced a book that would be prized for centuries.[64] However, it might more readily concur with his opinion that the entire series, which is altogether remarkable, is a monument to Clark's "ardour as a book-lover and as a great patron of the arts of the book."[65]

Clark's patronage of Nash was not limited to the Christmas book series and library catalogues. Only comparatively more modest are the elaborate Christmas cards which Nash printed for him for a dozen years. Nash's papers leave no indication of the price Clark was charged for these items. We can assume that it was high. Taking as their model the richly ornamented medieval manuscript, these cards present a rich typographical picture, the elements of which are heavy handmade paper, gothic type, and even rubrication and ornamentation.

There were commissions for other material as well—Easter cards, envelopes, stationery, and labels for the Library. Occasionally, Clark would have Nash print a special item, such as a deluxe edition of Robert Burns' *The Bonie Lass that Made the Bed to Me* (1927).

Clark was also a good customer for other Nash imprints, and he could be generous in his support of Nash's more ambitious projects with which he had no formal connection. For example, he was an early subscriber to the *Divine Comedy* before Nash had even begun to print the work.[66] Throughout the Twenties, Clark was always there when Nash needed him. Perhaps more significantly, he was often quite willing to extend his financial assistance when Nash did not particularly need it. The generous profits he allowed Nash, the prestige of his support, and, above all, his interest were of the greatest importance to Nash's career and the direction which it took. Had the Depression not interrupted this patronage and had Clark's untimely death not ended it, the last decade of Nash's career would have been quite different.

If William Andrews Clark, Jr.'s library was his playhouse, as A. Edward Newton suggested,[67] the library of William Randolph Hearst was a small toy in a very large playhouse, for San Simeon contained probably the largest collection of collections in private hands. Hearst specialized in nothing so much as the act of acquiring. Spending for several years an average of one million dollars annually on his acquisitions, he could boast of possessing some of the world's finest collections of armor, old silver, old furniture, stained glass, Gothic mantels, and Mexican saddles. These and other collections spilled over into the many rooms of the buildings at San Simeon. In this morass Hearst somehow found the space to assemble a comparatively modest library which, however, was displayed incomparably in a beautiful Gothic study. There one could find examples of fine bindings and of the printing of past and contemporary masters. Lacking in his book collecting was that relentless and thorough procedure which characterized his acquisition of other items. Hearst was a well-read man, but he had few of the tastes or instincts of the bibliophile. He was first and foremost a newspaperman, with the newspaperman's great respect for the power of the printed word and his indifference to its appearance.

Why, then, did Hearst decide to patronize America's leading exponent of the book beautiful? There were two reasons: Hearst's reverence for the memory of his parents and Nash's reputation as the most outstanding fine printer then at work. When Hearst decided to publish the life of his mother and father he wanted the books to be the best that money could produce, and the best, he determined, could come only from the shop of John Henry Nash.

Although Hearst and Nash had mutual friends and moved occasionally in the same circles, they probably did not meet before 1927, the year that Hearst decided to commission biographies of his mother and father. Through one of those fortuitous circumstances that graced Nash's career during the Twenties, Hearst's chief advisor in San Francisco, John F. Neylan, was a bibliophile and Nash's good friend. Whether Hearst first thought of employing Nash or not, once the decision was made, Neylan was able to give his wholehearted support to that decision. Neylan arranged for the initial meeting between Hearst and Nash, which was scheduled to be brief, but the two men liked each other at once, and a confrontation be= came a leisurely and friendly discussion.[68] The publisher and printer were to become good friends, in spite of, or perhaps because of, Nash's refusal to meet all Hearst's demands. Hearst wanted the bi= ography of his mother, the first of his two memorials, to include several family photographs, and he wanted it to be finished in a hurry. Nash had an aversion to working with photographs, and he refused to be hurried. An impasse seemed inevitable, but Hearst was in the hands of a master salesman. Nash convinced him that the book would be far more impressive without photographs and that, as a product of his shop, it was well worth waiting for. An agreement was drawn up which gave Nash a comparatively free hand in the production of the book. There were to be no photographs; the frontispiece portrait of Phoebe Apperson Hearst was to be etched after that photograph which, in the opinion of Hearst and his wife, best captured her likeness. Nash agreed to provide special paper, bearing alternately the watermarks "Hearst" and "Nash," and to maintain the high standards of his previous work. He was expected to produce a monumental piece of work. Nash was to have one year, from the date of the delivery of the manuscript, to complete the book. The edition was to consist of one thousand copies for which Nash was to be paid $40,000.[69]

The news of Nash's commission to print biographies of Hearst's parents was released to the press and to printing trade journals, and Nash made the most of the event by broadcasting it widely himself. This was his most expensive commission, and along with the work he did for William Andrews Clark, Jr., it made him the most gen= erously patronized fine printer of his time.

Hearst's reward was intended to be an inimitable and perfect book. In its technical execution, its opulence, and its uniqueness, it would achieve the quality of conspicuousness which Hearst craved. Keeping Hearst and the bookmaking community apprised of his preparation for the printing of this work, Nash left for Europe shortly after the agreement was drawn up in mid-April of the year 1927. Upon arriving, Nash proceeded to the Van Gelder paper mills at Appeldoorn near Amsterdam where he arranged for the fabrication of a lot of paper especially for the production of the book. Nash had already used, and had been completely satisfied with, the paper which that firm manufactured. For this book, however, the excellent product of Van Gelder was not sufficient. He wanted something extraordinary, something that could not be imitated. According to his own account, he stood over the vats while rags were being pulped and the stuff produced. At his suggestion, black rags were added to give the paper darkish threads and an unusual appearance.[70]

William Wilke, Nash's versatile artist-in-residence, executed the frontispiece, the ornamental borders, and the ingenious headbands that gave the keynote to each of the chapters in the biography. Nash selected as his type Cloister Light Face, one of his favorites, and incorporated into his typographical design the inevitable rule scheme. To encase this monument of fine printing, he turned over the sheets, which were printed in Germany[71] from electrotyped plates made in San Francisco, to one of Europe's finest binderies, the Leipzig firm of Hübel und Denck. Each of the one thousand copies of this book was bound in unbleached vellum with lettering and rules hand-stamped in gold. Finally, to protect the pages from dust, Nash had green fleece bags made to cover each bound volume. The result of this great enterprise—the most technically perfect book that American and Europan skill could produce—was the kind of superproduct that Hearst was able to appreciate. It was worthy of being collected.

Phoebe Hearst was equal to this royal attire, for her life had been a remarkably noble one. She was one of the great philanthropists of her era and, at the same time, one of the most unpretentious of women. The combination had made her widely revered. It was not her fault or Nash's that the author of her biography should be a person totally unfit to prepare the conscientious and serious study which her career and Nash's artistry deserved.

The fault was William Randolph Hearst's: first, in selecting "Annie Laurie," one of the most popular columnists working for him, to write the biography; and second, for not telling her, apparently, that she was writing a book and not an extended column. "Annie Laurie," otherwise known as Mrs. Winifred Black Bonfils, was a brilliant newspaper reporter. Her courage, tenacity, and intelligence had secured for her more than one exclusive story and a position of eminence in a highly competitive profession dominated by men. The basis of her popularity, however, was primarily her emotional approach to and analysis of the news. She knew, additionally, the fine art of adjusting facts. These were hardly qualifications for the undertaking of a serious biography. Perhaps, if she had taken the time, these weaknesses might have been eliminated. She thought she did not have the time, and the result was catastrophic. One of the most monumental books of modern times which contains the biography of a truly great woman was written in twelve days "in gushy prose, replete with errors—the work of a sob sister in a hurry."[72]

It was fortunate for everyone concerned with the production of this work that no one had the audacity to point out publicly these flaws at the time of its appearance. It was easier and safer to dwell upon the occasion—the appearance of a biography of a beloved lady —and the physical beauty of the book itself. The one thousand copies, none of which was for sale, were distributed as gifts to the friends of Hearst and his mother and to selected institutions and libraries. As with the Clark books, Nash was able to have certain of his own supporters placed on the mailing list as well. The recipients were appropriately impressed with their gift. Published comments about the book were always polite, frequently enthusiastic, and occasionally ebullient. Not surprisingly, the *San Francisco Examiner*, a Hearst newspaper, made the most exaggerated claim—that the book was one of the finest examples of printed matter in the world.[73]

Nash's friends in high places managed to turn the occasion of the appearance of this work, as they had of other Nash books, into a local celebration. At the suggestion of President Reinhardt of Mills College, a public showing of the book was held in the Art Gallery at Mills. The exhibition was formally opened on the evening of March 7, 1929, with a dinner followed by talks delivered by President Reinhardt ("Biography and Books"), Winifred Bonfils ("Materials for the Life of Phoebe Apperson Hearst"), and Nash ("The Making of the Book"). For one week, this modern miracle of fine printing was placed on exhibit and admired by a substantial number of viewers. An announcement of the event, written by Edward F. O'Day and printed by Nash, utilizes effectively some of the attractive and ingenious border designs of the original. The announcement contains, not surprisingly, some flattering words about the printer:

The completed text of this biography was wisely committed to the strong, expert hands of John Henry Nash—and what a book he has made of it! There can be no question that this *Life* will command a foremost position on those shelves that bibliophiles give to their collections of Nashiana. The Nash imprint is today famous throughout the world, and is steadily, quietly gaining a solidity of repute that has every appearance of typographical immortality. Let those who would know the reason for this study the volume in question.[74]

There is probably no more striking example of the dizzying heights reached by Nash's local reputation than this event. Indeed, when or where during the twentieth century has another book newly issued from the press had such a christening?

Hearst could not attend the ceremony. He was, no doubt, flattered by the event and the general accolades which the book received. Fond of Nash as well as impressed by his work, he would have unquestionably continued to be one of Nash's chief patrons had it not been for the Depression which occurred the year after the appearance of the biography of his mother. His financial reverses during the Thirties cut short his excursion into bibliographic fields, and Nash was to experience some difficulty even in holding Hearst to the agreement that Nash should also print the biography of Hearst's father. This work was not published until 1933.

THE LIBRARY

Promotion dominated every facet of Nash's career. Consistently effective, it was brilliantly so in his Library and Typographical Museum, for that collection brought Nash more public attention and admiration than any of his other accomplishments. At the same time, the Library and Typographical Museum was Nash's chief source of inspiration. Its formation was probably his proudest achievement and the fulfillment of a lifelong dream.

That dream, which was not fully realized until the Twenties, began when Nash was a youth in Canada and before he entered his apprenticeship. When asked, later, why he chose to become a printer, Nash would usually say that his decision was made in large part because of an uncle's library to which he was allowed complete access. As he turned the pages of the handsome volumes in this modest but well-selected collection and absorbed the intriguing variety of types, paper, and design, he felt something of the excitement of the miracle of printing.

Nash's exposure to that library not only determined him to enter the trade of printing; it initiated him as well into a lifelong study of the history of printing. The seriousness of his interest can be gauged in part by the fact that it survived the effects of the apprenticeship system, for the student-printer was not encouraged to study the history and great heritage of his craft. Rather, he was actually discouraged from doing so. Few master printers knew or cared about the work of the great printers and type designers of the past. It was the exceptional printing office that contained a reference collection of finely printed books. Ignoring the examples of the past, the printer took as his only precedent whatever typographical design was then in vogue. Artistic license was fused with the technical facility which was at the command of many printers at the time to produce the grotesque excesses which marred the appearance of printing during much of the nineteenth century.

Nash was a product of this tradition. His first employers in Toronto, Denver, and San Francisco were conventional firms and therefore indifferent and perhaps even hostile to his interest. E. D. Taylor of The Stanley-Taylor Company, who shared Nash's interest in the history of his craft, was in no position to encourage it extensively by example. Yet while Nash's interest in the history of printing was not nurtured by any forces with which he came in contact, Nash would not let it die. Certainly, Nash must have himself collected the first library on printing to which he could turn. His library at this time would have been modest. He lacked funds to indulge such a luxury, and he was probably uncertain as to what material he should try to acquire. There were no available models for this comparative novice to follow. He may have had access to the library of Charles A. Murdock, before the earthquake of 1906, and, following his association with Paul Elder and Company, he could at least have seen examples of fine printing, from the incunabula period to contemporary fine presses, which Elder sold in his shop.[75] Nash may or may not have had time to study them, for Elder's collection was never permanent. Elder was interested in selling books, not in collecting them. It was during his brief sojourn in New York City, from 1906 to 1909, that Nash saw for the first time the kind of library he wanted to develop. While in that city, Nash journeyed to Jersey City, New Jersey, to visit the recently formed Typographical Library and Museum of ATF and its Librarian Henry L. Bullen. That library remained his model throughout his long career.

Upon his return to San Francisco with Paul Elder and Company, Nash was placed in comparative isolation from his model, but at least he knew now what he wanted. Additionally, his subsequent association with Taylor, Nash & Taylor encouraged his collecting instincts. The Taylor brothers, especially Henry Taylor, were both students of the history of printing. For the first time Nash had as colleagues men who agreed with his belief that any reputable printing firm should contain a reference library as an integral part of its equipment. This singular example of accord during the firm's explosive career resulted in the formation of such a library. With obvious pleasure the partners announced in 1915 in the pages of the *TNT Imprint* the formal opening of their library. The announcement suggests something of the feeling of enthusiasm which permeated the event:

It is with feelings of pride and satisfaction that we can now formally announce that the library which we have been building as an essential part of our printing plant is finally completed. This room has been one of our dreams that we hardly dared hope would ever become an actuality, and in the fulfillment of which expectation and realization unite on equal ground.

It is remarkable that while the modern printer has seldom a library of any kind the old-time followers of the art made this one of the most prominent features of their establishments. Our idea in building and equipping this room has been not only to provide a consultation-room, supplied with works of reference and a stock of the best examples of our own product, but more particularly to house such a selection of books as would prove to be a continual source of inspiration.[76]

The collection was modest, to be sure, but it could boast of four Aldines, a Satori Press book dated 1537, and more numerous examples from such modern fine presses as the Chiswick Press, the press of William Morris, the Merrymount, Riverside, University, and DeVinne Presses, and the press with which the firm had its greatest affinity—the Doves Press. The significance of this library, which we may be tempted to regard as slight, can be evaluated more accurately only in the context of the time. In 1915, the existence of such a printer's library was unusual. It would continue to be so for several more years. Three years later, in 1918, in describing an encounter with a midwestern printer who had established a similar library, Henry L. Bullen, who knew a great deal about contemporary printers, still chose to entitle his account "And this Happened in America!"[77]

Nash could not, of course, take the collection with him when he left Taylor, Nash & Taylor for Blair-Murdock, and he was not at the latter company long enough to develop a similar collection there. Once he opened his own firm in 1916, one of his first policies was to form a reference collection as quickly as funds would allow. His library probably consisted at first primarily of gifts from other American printers with whom Nash had begun an exchange program quite early in his career. To this collection, which was probably substantial by 1916, Nash added the numerous items of Nashiana he had done for the several firms by whom he had previously been employed. Among the works he had purchased were several treatises. He mentions in particular Edmund G. Gress' *The Art and Practice of Typography* (1910), which he held in high regard.[78] He also owned several of the works of Theodore DeVinne, including the reprinting of Moxon's *Mechanick Exercises.*

What Nash really wanted, however, and felt that he most needed, were examples of fine printing from earlier centuries—the work of the master printers from the incunabula period to the mid-nineteenth century. Although Nash would probably be the last person to admit it, a statement by Frederic W. Goudy describes exactly his own purpose in collecting such a library:

It is in the early printed books that the printer may find the sort of help he needs; there all the elements of types, ink and paper and impression are present in pristine state, where the arrangement of the types is simple and direct, uninfluenced by the demands of commercialism.[79]

As his income increased, Nash's acquisition of such examples accelerated, and he assembled during the Twenties an outstanding collection of works of earlier master printers. The Appendix describes this collection.

At the same time, Nash began to visit other libraries, not only to inspect those books and manuscripts which were of interest to him, but also to formulate more clearly in his mind the kind of library he wanted. It is not surprising that his first visit to Europe in 1921 should have been occupied largely with tours of libraries, both public and private. Nash spent three days at the Vatican Library. His next stop was Florence, where he visited the famous private collection of Leo S. Olschki. In Paris, he inspected the Bibliothèque Nationale. In England, he saw the Bodleian Library, the Library at Eton College and, of course, the British Museum Library. He was deeply impressed by the Plantin Museum in Antwerp. Its careful and convincing re-creation of the firm as it had existed in the seventeenth century fascinated him. Nash took in nearly every detail of that establishment, and he was not to forget what he saw. Later, when he commissioned custom-made furniture for his own library, he took as his model for individual pieces items he had seen in the Plantin Museum.

Nash found time, of course, to visit bookshops and to make purchases for his library. During his first trip to Europe he was able to purchase a fine copy of Jenson's *Eusebius*. A brief trip to Europe in 1924 was occasioned by his receiving a cable from Amsterdam notifying him that a copy of the Heilbronn Bible of 1476 was on sale. He left immediately for England by ship, and to expedite the final lap of his trip, he flew from London to Amsterdam, at a time when the airplane was still considered to be a daring and dangerous means of transportation. Nash got his Bible. An equally spectacular, if comparatively less grueling, trip enabled Nash to obtain a copy of the Strawberry Hill printing of Thomas Gray's *Odes*. Receiving word from Los Angeles that a copy of this work was for sale there, he travelled all that night, arriving in that city early the next morning. The trip was well worth his efforts. He purchased the book for $25.[80]

In 1923, Nash claimed that his library contained 2,500 volumes (he must have meant items). By 1925, he was said to have spent $40,000 on his library.[81] Both calculations are probably high. Nash's generosity, however, in allowing access to his library is an established fact, and its limits were determined only by the dimensions of his quarters. It was to provide more space for his library that Nash moved to the new building on Sansome Street in 1925.

Leasing the entire sixth floor of this building which, although not his, was called the John Henry Nash Building, Nash finally had quarters worthy of his library. Effectively contrasted with the spartan simplicity of the composing room, the library's setting was sumptuous. Tall, open cases, flanking the walls, displayed Nash's books in all of their varied textures and colors. These provided an added richness to the appearance of the well-lighted room. A fireplace and a massive mantel, which Nash designed, dominated one end of the room. Chairs, tables, and cabinets, all custom-designed in English white oak, gave weight and opulence to the room. The center table alone was said to have cost Nash $1,000. Busts of Gutenberg and Franklin were placed in conspicuous locations. Oil portraits of Gutenberg, Bodoni, Morris, DeVinne, and others, done for Nash by Henry Raschen, decorated the walls.

The guest book, bound in a cover which formerly held a copy of the 1478 edition of Plutarch's *Lives*, was placed on one end of the center table. It was never untouched for long. Hundreds of persons signed their names in it. Among the guests were celebrities—Katherine Cornell, Brian Aherne, Ted Shawn, and H. L. Mencken can be mentioned—as well as serious book collectors. But the majority of Nash's visitors were persons who were neither celebrities nor book collectors. Students, ladies' clubs, printers, businessmen, and others from nearly every walk of life came by the hundreds. Nash's library was, for several years, a minor tourist attraction in San Francisco.

As for the natives, they began to take a real civic pride in Nash's library. Nash's trips to Europe and the booty he brought back with him were local news. For example, his extensive acquisitions made during his trip of 1927 were carefully itemized in the *San Francisco Examiner* and the *San Francisco Chronicle*.[82] Following his return from Europe in 1929, Nash was given a feature story by Gregor Duncan in the December 28 *San Francisco Call Bulletin*, entitled "He's the Type." In 1933, Nash was invited by a local radio station to give a talk about his library, an event which must have been the first of its kind.

Cordiality prevailed at the Nash library. Nell O'Day, Nash's Librarian, would set the mood by saying to the visitor, "Look around and make yourself at home,"[83] and indeed she meant it. Except for certain very rare items, the books were arranged on open shelves, and visitors were allowed to remove and inspect them. Nash usually stayed close to the composing room, but he would try at least to step across the hall and to greet as many of the library's visitors as possible. Attired in a linen working-smock, completely informal, displaying simplicity and directness, he delighted most of his visitors, many of whom had expected pretension, pomposity, and perhaps even arrogance from so renowned a man. But Nash's role in his shop and library was that of the simple craftsman, proud of his work, and eager to show it off. "Mr. Nash was so generous with his time that I felt guilty," wrote one visitor.[84] Another makes Nash, in his farewell comments, a most genial and eager host. "Come back soon," Nash urged, "come back whenever you want to, and bring your friends."[85]

So well-appointed a stage was used for other performances as well. Nash's annual Christmas parties were held in his library. Food and drink were served; jokes were told; and a man could feel that a library was as convivial a place as his club. Visiting dignitaries were entertained there. Printing organizations were invited to hold meetings there. The A. Edward Newtons were fêted there in 1931 at an elegant buffet supper. Nash would use nearly any pleasant occasion to display his library, which was probably his most brilliant promotional enterprise. To his credit, it may be said that it was not created and never totally used as such. In the displaying of his library, Nash's generosity was sincere, his pride natural, and his goals not completely unworthy. Certainly, they included the greater glory of John Henry Nash, but they also reflected a profound pride in his craft and an unselfish attempt to educate as many people as possible in the importance of printing and the pleasures to be derived from a knowledge of it. None of his fellow printers had tried so conscientiously in this manner to act on the advice of A. W. Pollard that "the greatest need is to spread more widely a knowledge and appreciation of the essentials of good printing."[86]

GIFTS

While Nash's Library and Typographical Museum was the instrument for his more public promotional enterprises, his gift publications were reserved for the private circle of clients and patrons whose support had made his success possible. Unlike most of his fellow printers, Nash had learned early the validity of the parable of the casting of bread upon water. At the cost of a relatively small investment, Nash was to reap generous returns. His gifts forged a strong link of appreciation, sympathy, and enthusiasm between his patrons and himself that was to remain sound until his retirement.

Nash began dispensing his gift books, pamphlets, and broadsides at the point in his career when he could least afford to do so. Yet he knew, from his experience with Taylor, Nash & Taylor in particular, that these were an effective form of advertisement. These gifts brought Nash new patrons and helped him to retain old ones. During the Twenties, when his stature was such that he no longer needed to advertise himself in this manner, he continued to do so. His natural impulses of generosity and self-aggrandizement would not allow him to abandon what had become one of his most pleasurable activities. Indeed, his increasingly prosperous financial state during the Twenties added to the opulence and elegance of these items.

Nash treated his gift printings as virtuoso pieces, and among them are some of his most spectacular productions. Their purpose is reflected in the grandiose typographical design which Nash applied to them. When subject matter is suited to design, these items can be truly impressive. This is not always the case, and for some of his gift printings Nash received his sharpest and most deserved criticism. However, it may be said of these works that they never lack interest and that, at the time of their appearance, they were eminently successful in achieving the promotional goal for which they were created.

One of the reasons for the continuing interest of several of these works is the evocative nature of their typography which, of course, is a reflection of Nash's interest in and knowledge of the history of printing. Nash often based his design on that of individual works of the past. His typefaces were usually those modelled on older typefaces. His ornaments were taken from his extensive collection of historical ornaments. His paper was nearly always handmade. Nash's gift items present an interesting series of studies in allusiveness.

Nash's first gift printing of the Twenties is a booklet published during the Christmas season of 1920. Entitled *Ecclesiastes or the*

Preacher, it uses Moyen Age Gothic, a type manufactured in France. Initial letters, patterned after those used in the 1485 printing of a *Roman de la Rose*, are printed in red. The rules are in blue, while the text is printed with very rich black ink. The printing of three colors on heavy handmade paper called for elaborate makeready, and the production of this work kept Nash's chief assistant, Joseph Faunt-LeRoy, on his toes. His efforts were worthwhile, for the booklet is most impressive. Among the several persons who congratulated Nash on this volume was FauntLeRoy himself, who termed it truly an epochal piece of printing.[87] From the eminent book-collector A. Edward Newton came the flattering opinion that Nash's *Ecclesiastes* was one of the most beautiful examples of printing he had ever seen.[88]

Nash's second substantial gift book appeared during the Christmas season of 1922. It is the Philip Wicksteed translation of Boccaccio's *Life of Dante*. Nash regarded this volume as one of his favorites, perhaps because it is the only one of his books for which he set all of the type.[89] The events which mark the publication of this work record an example of Nash's very successful advertising campaign and are described here as a model of a policy which he often applied. First of all, Nash printed an *Announcement*, which noted rather briefly that he had been given permission to print a new edition of the Wicksteed translation. This was followed by an *Apologia*, occasioned by unforeseen delays at the source in Europe where Nash had placed orders for the type and paper he had chosen for this work. Later in the year, when these materials had been shipped to him and he had completed this book, he printed an elaborate *Apologia Withdrawn!*, which pronounced the book's completion and imminent distribution. The *Apologia Withdrawn!* is quoted here in full, for it displays the Nash style of salesmanship which at once impresses, flatters, and intimidates. The *Apologia Withdrawn!* says:

This book I have completed with pride—and with relief! Pride, since that best defines the satisfaction of accomplishment; relief, because the ending of the task writes "finis" to a long chapter of mischance. The type, a recutting of Ratdolt, I ordered last year while in Italy; the water-marked paper, especially secured for this book, was made in Holland. A strike in the paper mill delayed delivery; a similar outburst of unionism in the foundry postponed for nine months the shipment of the type. And then, upon its receipt, it was dolefully brought to mind that the Italian alphabet lacks the "w," "y," and "k"! These sorts were forthwith ordered by cable. Finally, on consistent climax, the sorts proved to be higher than both the American standard and the original delivery, entailing further worry. And the limitations of my present establishment have delayed completion—restrictions that I hope may shortly be banished by the acquisition of the "Place on the Hill," [Nash is referring to his Berkeley home] or an equal home for unharried and peaceful pursuit of what is both my vocation and my hobby. Yet I look on the completed book as the most worthy of all that I have printed—perchance with the greater love inspired by harder travail. This book is my acknowledgment of the appreciation of a certain few. It is no venture in commercialism; its distribution will add no ciphers to my bank account. Nor is it a gift, creating an obligation. Rather is it a tangible expression of gratitude to those few whose kindly appraisal of my other efforts adds zest to the striving for higher attainment. And so, being bound neither by the conventions of gift-making nor the calculated economics of merchandising I have cheerfully disregarded established usage and made of each page what is to the eye of John Henry Nash a beautiful typographical picture. You will find no black spots in it to distract; no rivulets of white to lead the eye astray from sense and sequence. The relieving spots of color are placed with a designing reserve. I confess to have quite ignored the tyrannies of Noah Webster in the matter of breaking words. Other liberties with pompous precedent will reveal themselves to the discerning eye. For I am quite in accord with my good friend, Dr. George Watson Cole, the librarian of the Henry E. Huntington Library, who tells me in a treasured letter: "Some time ago I promised to send you a copy of my little pamphlet *The Extra Gill and the Full Quart Pot; A Bibliographical Study*. For a long time I was unable to lay my hands on it, but a copy has now turned up and I am hastening to send it to you before it again hides itself. I think, after reading it, you will agree with me that the modern printer is sadly handicapped in his work by a slavish adherence to the spelling laid down in the dictionaries. This allows him no flexibility in his work. In consequence there is an irregularity of spacing in the lines of modern books that greatly detracts from their appearance. Can we ever hope a return to the beauty of page shown by the spacing of the early printers?" It is more than a coincidence that in this book the unbroken typography assists the reader to meander leisurely with Boccaccio through the long sentences that so well convey his whimsical and ruminative narrations and philosophies. And here let me make mention of a rare thing—in the long hours I have devoted to setting up the type in this "Life of Dante" I have many times caught myself entirely diverted from the task in hand, absorbed in the text or in the thought it prompted. That is not usual for a printer, concentrated on the art and the mechanics of his work—let it be my own humble tribute to the charm of the book! I pray the possessor of this copy of "Trattatello in Laude di Dante" (commonly known as the "Life of Dante") that he do not part with it but rather cherish it as a personal message of gratitude. Not because it will doubt-less gain an appreciated value with the years (for I admit a satisfaction that some of my earlier books now bring a not inconsiderable premium) but be-cause it is an intimate expression to my friends of my own ideas of typo-graphy.

Dedicated to Charles W. and William Andrews Clark, Jr., this publication fully achieved its purpose. Its recipients were impressed not only with the work itself but also with the spirit which moti-vated its entire production. "It is superb-wonderful," said the Editor of *The Needle*, the house organ of the excellent Los Angeles print-ing firm of Young and McCallister, Inc., who continued: "In it the old art of book making lives once more."[90] The Dean of English typographers, George W. Jones, wrote Nash that "it is a long time since I have seen anything which expresses love and mastery of craft so successfully."[91] Stanley Morison included reproductions from the book in his *Modern Fine Printing* as examples of a very fine handling of the Inkunabula type.[92] Praise came from W. Irving Way, Jerome Kern ("Pray don't think it hyperbolic when I say that, to me, it is like a beautiful melody"), and Henry L. Bullen,[93] although Bullen had reservations about the legibility of the type. Bruce Rogers pre-sented additional criticism of the Inkunabula, but this was prefaced with warm praise for the "immaculately perfect" workmanship of the book. He pointed out the flaws in the Inkunabula, a recutting done in Italy of Ratdolt's roman type—its too wide spacing, the com-paratively inferior roman of Ratdolt, and the fact that the recutting should never have been reproduced in such large sizes which, he said, were too gross for anything but poster work.[94] But Bullen's and Rogers' were lone voices of dissension, and qualified dissension at that.

In producing this, his favorite gift book, Nash was extravagant. Not only was the cost to Nash about $35 a copy, but the work also took most of his free time for several months. Understandably, Nash's next gift printings were more modest. His 1924 printing of Bret Harte's *Heathen Chinee* is relatively subdued in appearance; perhaps for this reason Rogers described it as splendid and magnifi-cent.[95] Nash produced only two more gift books during the Twenties. The first was occasioned by the untimely death of Ray F. Coyle, the gifted artist who had done several ornaments and frontispieces for Nash. It is a commemorative volume and contains reproductions of six of Coyle's more typical illustrations which are very much in the Beardsley manner. Nash's final gift printing of the Twenties, the ultimate in luxury, is a handsome edition, published in 1929, of the *Psalms of the Singer David*. Nash worked on this book, very intermittently, for ten years. In its typographical design, it is evocative of the style of Ratdolt which Nash so admired for its sumptuousness and its suggestion of the rich manuscript page. Nash used the wide borders favored by Ratdolt, and he further relieved the weight of the heavy design and close composition by graying the ink. The paper, imported from Germany, presented one crucial problem—the presence of flint-like particles which damaged the plates from which the work was printed.[96] Yet the final result is technically perfect. A copy of this gift book was presented by Nash to each of the subscribers of his recently published monumental edition of the *Divine Comedy*. The incipit, "full of promotional honey" in the words of FauntLeRoy,[97] pays tribute to Nash's friends:

Here begins The Psalms of David now newly imprinted by John Henry Nash for his friends, and notably for his Jewish friends of San Francisco. This is a fitting occasion for a tribute to the men and women of San Francisco who proudly claim racial connection with the royal singer of Israel. Our city acclaims them for their distinguished patronage of music, art and letters, no less than for their charitable and philanthropic generosity. Let me add my individual acknowledgement, for to the Jews of San Francisco I owe a debt of friendship that can never be fully discharged.

Nash was careful to proclaim publicly the cash value on this gift which he calculated to be $50 a copy,[98] a figure that was probably not inaccurate at the time. His *Psalms* marks the apex of his work during a boom-decade that was about to collapse.

To the relatively few gift books which Nash printed are to be added his gift pamphlets, French-folds, and broadsides. Nash would accept nearly any occasion as an excuse for their production, as long as that occasion related in some manner to him. Mills College had bestowed upon him in 1923 the honorary degree of Master of Arts. For the next three years Nash presented handsome printings

The Tomoyé Press. Nash is standing on the extreme left.

The Tomoyé Press, ca. 1903. Nash is fourth from the left.

31 That the Peneian frond should breed the more
joy in the joyous Delphic deity
when it makes anyone athirst therefor.
34 From tiny spark flame follows hot and high:
after me better voices shall perchance
lift up such prayer that Cyrrha may reply.
37 Through different entrances to mortal glance
the world's lamp rises, but from out that station
where join three crosses with four circling bands
40 With a better course, with a better constellation
it comes conjoined, sealing with stamp more clear
and tempering mundane wax more to its fashion.
43 This entrance had almost made it evening here
and morning yonder; all was there aglow
while darkness overcast our hemisphere,
46 When, turned about toward the left-hand, lo!
Beatrice who was gazing on the sun:
never did eagle fasten on it so.
49 And just as ever from the former one
issues a second ray and upward flies,
like pilgrim turning homeward, journey done,
52 So did her act, informing through the eyes
mine own imagination, give me grace
to eye the sun beyond our wonted wise.
55 Much is permitted yonder, in this place
prohibited our powers, thanks to the spot
fashioned expressly for the human race.
58 Not long did I endure this, and yet not
so little but I saw it sparkling nigh,
as iron from the fire pours boiling hot;
61 And of a sudden day to day thereby
seemed to be added, as if He who can
had with another sun adorned the sky.

LINE 31
Since Daphne (the laurel) is daughter of the river-god Peneus, the bay-leaf is called Peneian.

LINES 34-36
The Poet expresses the modest hope that better poets may some time be animated by his example to treat more worthily of his great theme. Cyrrha, ancient port of Delphi, here stands by metonymy for Apollo.

LINES 37 FF.
Here the action begins. The place of starting is the Earthly Paradise at the summit of the Mount of Purgatory. The time is Wednesday of Easter week, 1300, at noon. It is now some three weeks after the vernal equinox, when the circles of the celestial Equator, the Zodiac, and the Equinoctial colure cross the circle of the Horizon,—a moment when the influence of the sun, merging with that of Aries (the best constellation), is most favorable. As the sun rises to mortals through a different gate every day, the conditions cannot be exactly those of the vernal equinox, but almost all the southern hemisphere is lighted and the northern correspondingly darkened. As the Mount of Purgatory is in the center of the southern hemisphere, it follows that the hour is nearly that of noon "yonder," while "here," in Italy, it is evening. At Jerusalem, the center of our hemisphere, opposite Purgatory, it is midnight.

LINE 55
As in line 44, "yonder" refers to the garden at the top of the Mount of Purgatory; "in this place," to the actual

William Andrews Clark, Jr., Nash's chief patron.

ALL FOR LOVE

or, the World well Lost: A Tragedy

By JOHN DRYDEN

*Facile est verbum aliquod ardens (ut ita dicam) notare:
idque restinctis animorum incendiis irridere.* CICERO.

San Francisco:

Printed for William Andrews Clark, Jr.

by John Henry Nash

1929

The most opulent of the Clark Christmas books.

N *Account with* JOHN HENRY NASH

447 Sansome Street, San Francisco : *Telephone Sutter 6872*

December 28, 1929

Mr. William Andrews Clark, Jr.
2205 West Adams Street
Los Angeles, California.

To Planning and Printing 250 copies ALL FOR LOVE)
  By John Dryden   )
With 250 books in Facsimile of the First Edition)...$37,500.00

By Check November 20, 1929 ....10,000.00
                                                      $27,500.00

These books (facsimile and reprint) are double the size
of other Christmas books in composition, number of pages,
art work, facsimile plates, copper etchings, double frontispiece and headbands, and the color plates of the Library
murals, which had to be made abroad. *Paid*

And the most expensive: The bill.

The Nash Library.

The Nash home in Berkeley: The rewards of success.

BIBLIA SACRA

VULGATAE EDITIONIS
SIXTI V ET CLEMENTIS VIII PONT. MAX.
AUCTORITATE RECOGNITA

A
IOANNE HENRICO NASH
ACCURANTIBUS CALIFORNIENSIUM SANCTAE CLARAE
ET SANCTI FRANCISCI UNIVERSITATUM
QUIBUSDAM DOCTORIBUS
EDITA

SANCTI FRANCISCI
M. CM. XXX. II.

The title page of Nash's uncompleted *magnum opus*.

"Forty Years at the Case"
Friends of John Henry Nash celebrate the
fortieth anniversary of his entry into printing
Nash Library, San Francisco
March 17, 1927

Homage to Nash. Seated left to right are Bruce Brough, Frank Abbott, John Kitchen, Jr., Nash, Howard Griffith, Haywood H. Hunt, and John Hogan. Standing at the far left and right are William Wilke and Joseph FauntLeRoy.

to each of the members of the graduating classes of that institution. Following the tragic death in 1926 of George Sterling, a close friend of Nash's, he printed a dignified broadside bearing a touching eulogy by H. L. Mencken, who was in Nash's library when the news of Sterling's death arrived. When Nash's printing of *El Toison de Oro: the Golden Fleece* was awarded first prize in 1926 in the Graphic Arts Leaders of America Competition, he printed an elaborate appreciation, entitled *An Anthology of Effort*; this he dedicated to all those persons who had helped him in its production. His 1927 Christmas card, a reprinting of Edward H. Hamilton's sentimental salute, *A Toast to the Ladies*, is impressive in appearance. However, it is Nash's accompanying message—that he regarded Hamilton's comments as an effective antidote to the negativism and sordidness of such current fiction as *Oil* and *Elmer Gantry*—which shows the master salesman's perfect sense of timing. The influential "Annie Laurie" thought Nash's gesture a beautiful one.[99] *Ad Age*, the journal of the San Francisco Advertising Club and Better Business Bureau, was rhapsodic in its appreciation:

Like a mellow, softly-lighted stained glass window in a corner of a great cathedral, Mr. Nash has given this masterpiece of sentiment a worthy setting, where it may serve as a shrine for those ideals of womanhood which almost every man cherishes or hopes to hold some day toward those nearest and dearest to him.[100]

Nash's vacation announcements became legend. What other printer, to please as well as to inform, had printed in four colors, on hand-made paper, and in impeccable presswork, an announcement of the closing of his shop? An invitation to a Nash party was worthy of collecting. His Christmas cards were seldom less than spectacular.

Nash's gifts, the result of a desire to please and to impress, touched his contemporaries deeply. They were proud to know so eminent a man, but they were even more flattered that they should be the recipients of such remarkable works produced "for the Joy of Doing." Many of these persons developed a respect and an appreciation for fine printing that had not existed before and a willingness to pay handsomely for it.

Among these new converts were many businessmen and financiers, men who had not previously regarded printing as anything more than a means of transmitting entertaining or useful facts and opinions. Perhaps the greatest factor contributing to Nash's success was his ability to attract the attention of these men. He did so at a perfect time, for the Twenties was the age of the businessman whose support helped to mold the successful combination of Nash's career of printing, patronage, and promotion.

Chapter V

THE THIRTIES: DEPRESSION AND DECLINE

NEITHER BY TEMPERAMENT nor by experience was Nash a person who could be discouraged easily. If the news of the October 29, 1929, stock market crash seriously alarmed some of his friends, it did not unduly upset Nash. His great patrons, William Andrews Clark, Jr., and William Randolph Hearst, were still wealthy men. Other clients were still willing to pay his prices; his reputation was still secure. Nash's optimism seemed justified, on the whole, during the years 1930 and 1931. The following year, however, he was forced to face the realities of the existence of the Depression. By 1933 and 1934 he was in financial trouble. Nash's finances improved somewhat during the last years of the Thirties, but the spirit of the Twenties had been irrevocably lost and with it the source of much of his inspiration.

The year 1930 was busy and prosperous for Nash. The printing of William Andrews Clark, Jr.'s Christmas book for that year, Robert Louis Stevenson's *Father Damien*, brought Nash $22,375. He completed for Clark as well another volume in the series of the library catalogues. As usual, Nash also produced for Clark an elaborate and costly Christmas card. Clark had become an uneasy patron, it is true. The price of copper had not recovered from the plunge it had taken earlier, and the prudent Clark had advised Nash in the spring of 1930 that he might not publish a Christmas book.[1] He had changed his mind, however, and there was nothing depressed about the appearance of *Father Damien* which is in the tradition of the Clark Christmas book series. The behavior of Hearst was somewhat more alarming, for he seemed reluctant to give Nash firm instructions to proceed with the printing of the biography of Hearst's father, and Nash could have used the $40,000 which had been agreed upon as the price.

If the attitude of his two greatest patrons was somewhat disquieting, that of the Book Club of California must have been reassuring, for Nash printed two expensive works for the Club in 1930. The first had its inception in the salad days of 1928. That year the President of the Club, Alfred Sutro, presented to the Club an incomplete copy of the *Nuremberg Chronicle* with the understanding that it would be broken up so that at least one leaf of the original would accompany each copy of Nash's printing of Henry L. Bullen's study of the work—its origins, form, and influence. The Club's publication is elaborately illustrated with twenty-four reproductions of the original woodcuts. The title page contains a reproduction of the original Gothic title lines. The work is printed on Van Gelder paper and bound in a special marbled paper which Nash had obtained, fittingly, from Nuremberg. Sold to members at $15, $25, or $35 a copy, depending upon how many original leaves were inserted, the book, neither in its appearance nor price, reflects the hard times into which it was born.

As solicitous as Nash was of the Book Club's *Nuremberg Chronicle*, he lavished on the other Book Club publication of 1930 all the attention of which his shop was capable. His concern in this matter was shared by the Book Club's directors, for they were also anxious that the Club's publication of *Mr. Strahan's Dinner Party* should impress, indeed overwhelm, its author, the famous bibliophile from Philadelphia, A. Edward Newton, whose reputation and prestige were then at their height. Newton already knew the Club and Nash, on whose private mailing list he had been placed in 1925, and said that he was impressed by both.

Possibly the visit to San Francisco early in 1930 of Newton's daughter, Caroline, who was fêted at Nash's shop, gave the Book Club's directors the idea of publishing a product of the mighty triumvirate of Newton, Nash, and the Club. Newton was approached and asked to submit a manuscript of his choice for publication. He acceded with his short play entitled *Mr. Strahan's Dinner Party*, written originally to be read by him on the occasion of his inauguration in September, 1930, at Litchfield, England, as President of the Johnson Society. This additional association whetted the interest of the Book Club's directors and of Nash even more. Newton was promised that he could expect something very special in the printing of his play. In Nash's opinion that promise was fulfilled. Nash said of *Mr. Strahan's Dinner Party* that the book was the best thing he had ever done.[2]

Newton was properly impressed. At least, he was gracious enough to say he was. As usual, Nash's technical performance is laudable, and, additionally, the typographical design is appealing, but then, what book which was said to show the influence of Updike, Rogers, and the Whittingham Press[3] could be less than delightful?

Neither Nash nor the Book Club would be able to indulge themselves in such luxury for much longer. Nash certainly expended on the Newton book more in time and material than could be recompensed by the Club. The quotation, at $14 a copy,[4] is even less impressive when we find that this figure also includes the printing of letters and brochures which advertise the book. Additionally, Nash was to be paid as usual, only as copies of the book were sold.

In better times, such considerations would have been regarded by Nash as trifles, and even in 1930 he could not accept the fact that the end of the good times of the Twenties was permanent. Nash maintained the pattern of his career, producing the same type of material and at the same tempo. He continued to be obsessed with perfection and to exact it from his assistants.

The year 1931 began badly but ended well for Nash. In February, Clark wrote him that he would probably not commission a Christmas book that year.[5] Nash journeyed to Los Angeles to try to change his mind, but Clark was adamant because he was really alarmed. The copper business was "shot to hades" he wrote Nash in August, and he explained that he already had several expensive obligations to honor.[6] There were, however, two more volumes of the Oscar Wilde catalogue to print, and Clark asked Nash to prepare a Christmas card for him—an attractive printing of Henry Wadsworth Longfellow's poem *Christmas Bells*. Hearst maintained an ominous silence.

That phenomenon of the book world during the Depression, the Limited Editions Club of New York City, offered Nash support in 1931. Begun in 1929, just before the crash, it had been able to maintain most of its 1,500 members during the lean years that followed. Founded upon the belief that there was a market for attractively printed and illustrated classics of literature, the Club was also interested in providing commissions for fine printers throughout the world. The printers of the first series of books were all Americans.

Nash was asked to contribute to the series, and negotiations went smoothly enough at first. The Club's director, George Macy, even placed an announcement in the April 6, 1929, *Publishers' Weekly* (page 1722) that Nash would definitely design and print an edition of Edgar Allan Poe's *The Narrative of Arthur Gordon Pym.*

He did not. The reason is probably that the illustrator of the book, René Clark, was Macy's choice and not Nash's. Nash had very definite views about appropriate illustrations. Furthermore, he was not accustomed to collaboration. His own illustrators were well trained in obedience. Reluctantly, therefore, Macy announced to Club members that Nash would not print the Pym book. The reason given was that Nash was unwilling to print on the dead white paper which Clark insisted upon using.[7] In declining to do the Poe book, Nash was denied the honor of being associated in that remarkable first series with Updike, the Goudys, Cleland, Dwiggins, Rudge, Marchbanks, the Grabhorns, and others. Nash would not have been much concerned. He did not particularly relish sharing honors.

It is an indication of Nash's popularity and reputation that again, in 1931, Macy approached him, this time allowing Nash to choose his own illustrator. Nash selected William Wilke. Edward O'Day, another San Franciscan, was invited to prepare the Introduction to the work which Nash selected to print—Benjamin Franklin's *Autobiography*. This, Nash's first book for the Limited Editions Club, was a resounding success. It was voted first place in a popularity poll of Club members for the 1931–1932 series,[8] and it was selected by the American Institute of Graphic Arts as one of the Fifty Books of the year for 1932.[9]

Nash could not resist the opportunity in 1931 of commemorating the twenty-fifth anniversary of the San Francisco earthquake and fire of 1906. Nor could he do so meanly. His printing for this occasion of St. Bonaventura's *Life of St. Francis of Assisi*, the city's patron saint, is an impressive—and probably an expensive—affair. Using fifteenth-century models, Nash evokes in the *Life* the richness and feeling of craftsmanship of the incunable book. Printed on German wood-block paper, his Moyen Age Gothic type is embellished with massive initials which Nash had only recently acquired during a trip to Spain.[10] Priced at $20 or $50 (the more expensive edition is bound in Gregorian chant manuscript sheets) the work is completely in the tradition of Nash's creations of the Twenties. Whether Nash could really sell many copies of this work is questionable. That he should produce such a work at all in 1931 bears testament to his faith—or folly.

These works and lesser commissions—for stationery, Christmas cards, the usual broadside testimonials, and the like—made the year 1931 good if not outstanding. The Christmas card he printed for Mrs. Estelle Doheny is extravagant; so was its price if she did indeed pay $25,000 for an edition of 1,000 copies as is rumored.[11] Nash still felt sufficiently expansive to issue one of his famous broadside vacation announcements, and he still retained a sense of humor. In his 1931 vacation announcement Nash reproduced the famous picture of the bookreading machine found in *Le Diverse et Artificiose Machine del Capitano Agostino Ramelli Paus* (1588). The accompanying text, however, described it as a proofreading device which he had just perfected. The joke was not universally comprehended; Nash received letters of congratulations for having produced so worthwhile an invention! His invitation to his annual Christmas party, entitled "Away with Depression," continued his good mood.

Perhaps one source of this mood was the honors which he continued to receive. In 1931, he was asked by the N. W. Ayer & Son, Incorporated, to be one of five judges who were to select the five newspapers produced in the United States which, in their opinion, had achieved the greatest typographical and printing excellence. Two western newspapers were among the winners—the Portland *Oregonian* and the *Long Beach Sun*—but the first prize went to the *New York Herald Tribune*. The event took place in Philadelphia, and Nash used the occasion to visit the Newtons. They were gracious hosts, and Nash enjoyed himself thoroughly.

Philadelphia was not alone in paying tribute to Nash. From Jersey City, New Jersey, came the announcement that to the series of stained glass windows made by Tiffany's, which are devoted to famous printers and presses and which adorned the Typographical Library and Museum, had been added one dedicated to Nash. He was in distinguished company. Only two other living printers—Bruce Rogers and George W. Jones—had been so honored.

In May, the Newtons returned the Nashes' visit. Their presence in San Francisco revitalized the somewhat lagging spirits of that city's bibliophilic citizenry. Nash, the Book Club of California, the Bohemian Club, and others, vied with each other "to spell HOS-PITALITY with large letters."[12] If the Newtons kept a tally sheet, Nash must certainly have won the contest. Who else in San Francisco, for example, could offer the Newtons hospitality not only of that city but also of Hearst's San Simeon and the promise of sleeping there in Cardinal Richelieu's bed? Whether or not the Newtons achieved that station is not recorded, but they must certainly have begun to feel the full weight of western hospitality. The dinners held for them by the Book Club of California and the Bohemian Club on May 12 and 13 were resounding successes, but Nash's smaller buffet supper held in his Library on May 11 was the most talked about. For one thing, what invitation could excel or even equal that which Nash prepared for this occasion? It was a broadside containing, in addition to the invitation itself, an elegant reproduction in color of the famous picture of Dr. Johnson waiting in Lord Chesterfield's anteroom. The roster of guests was equally impressive, consisting of Flodden W. Heron, Richard M. Tobin, William Randolph Hearst, John McCormack, Edward L. Doheny, Dr. A. S. W. Rosenbach, Dr. and Mrs. Robert G. Sproul, Dr. Aurelia Reinhardt, and, of course, the inevitable Albert Bender.

If Newton had arrived in San Francisco two months earlier, he would, no doubt, have been present at an even more impressive ceremony—the cornerstone laying and blessing on March 12, of Nash's new $100,000 home. Situated on a six-acre site in the Berkeley hills and designed by Nash's friend, the eminent architect Mark Daniels, the mansion was one of the area's most handsome and expensive homes. Nash's invitation to this affair was equal to the occasion, including a large handsomely printed map providing the directions to his home. At the event itself, nearly two hundred guests were present. Officiating were Archbishop Edward J. Hanna, who blessed the house, Leland W. Cutler, Mark Daniels, Roy Folger, and Edward F. O'Day. John McCormack was to have sung, but could not be there. Nash did not forget his fellow printers. In the audience were Haywood H. Hunt, Joseph FauntLeRoy, Paul and Charles Fay, Alfred B. Kennedy, John B. Kennedy of Kennedy-ten Bosch, and John J. Johnck. All of Nash's colleagues at the ceremony were probably as impressed as was John B. Kennedy, who wrote later to Nash: "Never did I dream I would witness the miracle of the most prominent men in the community traveling miles to pay tribute to a printer."[13]

That same month it was reported in the *Pacific Printer and Publisher* that Nash had recently purchased a copy of the 1501 Aldine *Virgil*. The price he was said to have paid was $1,500.[14] If anyone seemed determined to ignore the Depression in the bleak year of 1931, that person was Nash.

If Nash's actions during 1931 seemed to indicate that he was beyond the reach of the Depression, his announcement the following year—that he was about to publish an edition of the Bible which would sell at a very high price—suggests that he was either financially independent or financially irresponsible.

What fine printer has not dreamed one day of producing as his *magnum opus* an edition of the Bible? As one of the greatest literary achievements of mankind, as a holy scripture of three great religions, and as a book already produced by several of the greatest printers of the past, it has strong appeal. In Nash's own time, Cobden-Sanderson and Rogers crowned their illustrious careers with Bibles. Nash was not to be outdone. To produce a Bible had been one of his earliest aspirations, and as early as 1921 he began to make public pronouncements of his determination to achieve this goal.[15]

As events developed, Nash's more mundane career proved to be an obstacle. He was too busy and his shop was too small for him to carry on his regular business and the printing of so large a work, but he never abandoned his dream and continued to make plans, although rather sporadically and tentatively. With the decrease in work brought about by the Depression, he seemed finally to have the time, which he may have felt was running out, for he was no longer a young man, and he calculated that the project would take several years. He must certainly have felt a sense of urgency in getting on with the job.

Typically, Nash's first thoughts were not of costs, which would be substantial, but of the appearance of his great Bible. As the culminating work of his long and distinguished career it was worthy of his best efforts. Above all, he wanted it to be unique, to be something quite different from all other Bibles previously printed. To this end, he considered manufacturing a new typeface designed specifically for his own Bible. He turned for assistance to ATF, whose types he had used so effectively in the past. At first he rejected his favorite typeface, ATF's Cloister Light Face, as having already been used in several of his best books, including his *Divine Comedy* and his *Life and Personality of Phoebe Apperson Hearst*. Henry L. Bullen's suggestion that he use a type of the Serpentis style was also unsatisfactory.[16]

Both Bullen and Nash returned to Cloister Light Face, hoping that with certain modifications it would be appropriate. The principal problem was that the capitals were too obtrusive for use in the printing of a text replete with capitals. Experiments were made to modify the existing design. A combination of sixteen-point text with fourteen-point capitals was tried and rejected. The next experiment, which was Nash's suggestion, employed fifteen-point capitals on a sixteen-point body. This modification and a recutting of the capitals to condense their width and to make them slightly heavier seemed to correct the original weaknesses.[17]

Sample proofs using the modified types were run by Nash in his shop, and he seemed satisfied with the results. However, he was reluctant to commit himself yet to the use of Cloister Light Face. One reason for his hesitancy was his interest at the same time in using Bruce Rogers' Centaur type. Rogers had inadvertently put the idea into Nash's head when he offered to sell the original matrices of his Centaur to Nash in the spring of 1930.[18] The possible use in his Bible of the Centaur, which he had always admired, appealed to Nash. However, the sale did not take place. By December of 1930, Nash had definitely made up his mind to use Cloister Light Face.[19]

His paper would again come from the Van Gelder mills. Binding would be the best that craftsmanship could produce. Composition and presswork would, as always, maintain the highest standards. Nash decided that no ornamentation would be used other than a simple rule scheme. His perfect book was to be in the typographical tradition of his *Divine Comedy*, and his works about Cobden-Sanderson.

In his search for the unique, Nash rejected the King James Version for the text of his Bible. It had already been used by Baskerville, Cobden-Sanderson, and Rogers. Nor would he accept other Protestant versions, in spite of the promise of substantial backing from certain Protestant groups.[20] The Latin Vulgate appealed to him most, for the reasons outlined in the *Prospectus*. In his opinion, no printer had produced a Vulgate as a great typographical picture since Gutenberg. He felt that Latin more than English made such a picture possible, and he believed that the Vulgate was of far more significance historically than the King James Version or subsequent versions. Nash does not mention another and perhaps the most important reason: the printing of the Vulgate presented him with the greatest challenge.

Thus, in the midst of a serious depression in Protestant America, Nash announced his decision to print an expensive edition of the official Latin version of the Roman Catholic Bible. So apparently foolhardy a decision surprised no one who knew Nash. His career had already borne testimony to his willingness, indeed to his preference, to assume the seemingly impossible; "the line of least resistance," he had written, "has never seemed to me the best line between two points."[21]

However, Nash was not without perception. The church was not only eternal; it was also wealthy. There were devout and affluent Roman Catholics in America, several of whom were numbered among Nash's own clientele in San Francisco. With this group Nash's recent blessing from the Pope especially recommended him. In selecting the Vulgate Bible, Nash turned hopefully to a patron as steadfast as the rock on which it stood—the Roman Catholic Church.

There were difficulties in choosing this patron. The Church's official endorsement of his Bible would be difficult, if not impossible, to obtain unless the text in Nash's printing were totally acceptable. For instructions in proper protocol—and, incidentally, to relieve himself of the heavy burden of responsibility for proofreading the Latin text—Nash turned to friends at the Jesuit Universities of San Francisco and Santa Clara. Through the good offices of the Provincial of the Province of California, Father Joseph M. Piet, it was

arranged that the two universities would assume the responsibility
for the accuracy of the Latin text. Under these conditions, Nash
was able to obtain as well the permission of the Archbishop of San
Francisco, the Most Reverend Edward J. Hanna, to publish the
Bible under his imprimatur. What Roman Catholic of San Francisco,
of California, or of the United States would not be moved at seeing
on the title page of so beautiful an edition of the Vulgate the imprint
"Sancti Francisci"?

Nash was not satisfied with having met these requirements. He
saw the production of his Vulgate as a great religious drama and
considered the possibility of having the type blessed before it was
used in the printing of the Bible. He wrote to Henry Bullen asking
if there were a precedent for such a ceremony. The answer was
"no" but why not establish one.[22] Nash was most willing to comply
and made tentative arrangements with ATF for the manufacture of
new types and an oak or pine box of suitable appearance to house
them during the blessing ceremony.[23] On March 11, the official
announcement of the launching of the project was made by Archbishop Hanna.[24] A little later, Nash spoke about his Bible over a
local San Francisco radio station. "The occasion was probably
unique," said the *Pacific Printer and Publisher*, "in that a printer
was asked to give an address regarding his own work."[25]

Meanwhile, however, Nash had become increasingly aware of the
need for reliable support for so expensive and ambitious an enterprise. Individual Roman Catholic clients as well as the existing group
of collectors of Nash imprints seemed to insure the necessary support. However, the former group was untried and a relatively unknown quantity and the latter had already been diminished by the
effects of the Depression. For these reasons, Nash began to think of
the advisability of one patron's assuming the entire cost of the
work. Ideally, such a patron would be a wealthy, Roman Catholic
bibliophile. In Mrs. Edward L. Doheny of Los Angeles, Nash
thought he had found his person. Widely known as a generous bene-
factress, a devout Roman Catholic and a serious collector of books,
she seemed to be the perfect candidate. Additionally, she was interested in modern fine printing and knew and admired Nash's
work.

In opening his campaign to secure Mrs. Doheny's patronage, Nash was able, as usual, to secure the assistance of men in high places. He asked John McCormack and A. Edward Newton to write to her in support of his Vulgate. Newton's letter, a copy of which is in the Nash Archives, is an eloquent endorsement. Within a month of receiving Newton's letter, Mrs. Doheny was confronted in her Los Angeles home by Nash himself. Excellent salesman that he was, he came well prepared with samples and arguments. Mrs. Doheny was shown sheets of his Van Gelder paper, and Nash explained to her that if she should decide to support his project, the paper would carry her special watermark, just as for other impressive works it had displayed the watermarks of Clark and Hearst. He reminded her of the glory which had immortalized the names of great patrons of the past. He pointed out that books, being mobile objects, survive as memorials more satisfactorily than stationary structures or even good works. As a case in point, he predicted that the Christmas books he had done for William Andrews Clark, Jr. would far outlive Clark's expensive mausoleum and his patronage of the Philharmonic Orchestra. "Fire, earthquakes, floods and other disasters may overcome one part of the world or another," he wrote to her, "but there is reasonable assurance that copies will survive somewhere and keep his [Clark's] name alive."[26] Should she decide to sponsor the printing of Nash's Vulgate, of which he planned to print at least one thousand copies, Mrs. Doheny was being offered as many chances of immortality.

Shortly after his return to San Francisco, Nash sent her an elaborately printed broadside which accompanied what he said was the first set of printer's rough stone proofs of the title page and the first two pages of the text of his Bible. These he dedicated to this "outstanding Catholic laywoman, civic leader and philanthropist."[27]

By 1932, when the official *Prospectus* was sent out, Mrs. Doheny had not yet apparently accepted the signal honor which Nash had offered her. Nash, therefore, returned to his original and usual scheme of relying on individual subscriptions. The *Prospectus* is impressive and persuasive. Its four pages of "Explaining the Undertaking and Showing the Importance of the Vulgate" and its two pages of text, taken from the Book of Genesis, project authority and dignity. The typographical scheme, which is identical to that which was to be used in the Vulgate itself, is, as Nash had promised, subdued, relying for its effect primarily upon the quality of composition and presswork and the use of good ink and paper. Only a simple rule scheme and paragraph marks printed from Inkunabula type, used to offer a contrast to the Cloister Light Face of the text, provide ornamentation.

Nash's greatest enterprise did not advance beyond the *Prospectus*. It was not lack of subscriptions that terminated it, however, even at the price of $1,000 a set. When Nash told his supervisor Joseph FauntLeRoy to proceed with the printing of the Bible in the same manner employed in the printing of the *Divine Comedy*—that is, two pages at a time—FauntLeRoy replied that the undertaking was too ambitious without the addition of equipment.[28] Nash acquiesced with surprisingly little objection. The Vulgate was abandoned, and Nash's greatest dream remained unfulfilled.

Nash suffered a rude awakening from another dream in 1932, when the publication of a book scheduled to be printed by him for the Book Club of California was cancelled. The villain of this piece was the Depression, which had by that year taken its toll of Club membership. In spite of its reduced fortunes, the Club still felt a strong responsibility to give all the support at its command to California's fine printers. To cut costs and to maintain its shaky financial state, the Club initiated some new policies. Subscribers to its books were asked to make a substantial down payment with their orders, or were advised that unless a certain number of orders was received the book would not be published. The Club had lost money in 1931 on *The Santa Fé Trail to California 1849–1852*, which was priced at $30 a copy. Now regarded as one of the Club's most important publications, the work was simply too expensive for the time. Caution became the Club's motto. When, in 1932, it was decided to commission Nash to print an edition of H. H. Hart's *The Hundred Names: a Short Introduction to the Study of Chinese Poetry*, Club members were advised that at least half the 300 copies of the edition would have to be spoken for before actual production could begin. Only seventy-two orders were received, and the project was abandoned.[29] "This may well be worth the doing," one member replied in a typical reaction, "but I should have to know much more before spending $15 these days."[30]

The news from Clark was equally discouraging. Nash had counted upon Clark to resume the Christmas book series which had been interrupted the year before. Reluctant to leave the initiative to Clark, Nash used the visit to his library in March, 1932, of members of the Stratford-Upon-Avon Festival Company as a ploy. Where, Nash reported the actors as having enquired, was a work of Shakespeare among the Clark Christmas books? Nash repeated the question and urged Clark to consider selecting one of Shakespeare's plays to be printed as his 1932 Christmas book.[31] Nash's letter to Clark which contained this request had crossed in the mail with one from Clark with an entirely different message. Clark advised Nash in his letter that he had decided again not to have a Christmas book made. The best that he could promise was that he might get a Christmas card out.[32]

In Clark's retirement in 1932 from the role of patron, Nash had finally comprehended the full meaning of the Depression. For the first year during his association of over ten years with Clark, Nash would not be printing a book for his chief benefactor. Nash's reaction to this news was complaint. His situation had become such, he wrote to Clark, that he had begun again to take in commercial printing, which, he said inaccurately, he had not touched for years.[33]

Nash printed only one substantial book that year—Catherine L. Phillips' history of early San Francisco entitled *Portsmouth Plaza*. It was well reviewed,[34] and its physical beauty was noted.[35] This commission provided a bright spot in an otherwise dark year. However, the best news Nash received in 1932 was the instruction from William Randolph Hearst for him to proceed with the long-delayed printing of the biography of Senator Hearst.

Nash was probably happy to leave San Francisco for his annual summer vacation at Clark's lodge in Montana. His vacation broadside for the year 1932 shows a man who, for the first time, had grown disillusioned and bitter. It is an interesting and revealing publication, and the poem it bears, probably written by Edward F. O'Day, deserves to be quoted here in full:

A PRINTER DREAMS A TERRIBLE DANCE OF DEATH

I had a dream—it was a dreadful dream—
Where Things were as they Are, not as they Seem.
Methought a Holbein Dance of Death took life
And all his skeletons in horrid strife
To mournful strain and most funeral stave
Did pirouet upon an antique grave.
Of one nearby who watched in grief profound
I begged that he this nightmare might expound.

Quote he, "These are those printers of today
Who have no souls to animate their clay.
Wandered afar from standards of their craft,
Their puny minds with money-making daft,
They think of types as cost-accounting things,
And spurn the work that no huge profit brings.
Unto your vision, since you still can dream,
They're offered as they Are, not as they Seem."

"And whose the grave whereon with horrid din
They dance this rout of ribaldry and sin?"
My shadowy neighbor heaved a heavy sigh.
"Alas," he said, "it is the tomb where I
Was laid to rest some centuries ago—
A place of rest no longer but of woe."
"And you are—?"
                "Gutenberg," he cried, and fled . . .
The printers danced, not knowing they were dead.

                                    John Henry Nash, Printer

During his remaining six years as a San Francisco printer, from 1933 to 1938, Nash was not able to accommodate himself very successfully to the Depression. To his credit, it may be said that he tried and with some ingenuity and success, but there were always setbacks to counterbalance advances, and Nash was no longer young or in good health. He lost in the spring of 1933 the nearly indispensable services of Joseph FauntLeRoy when his chief assistant for fifteen years decided to retire from printing to take up orange-growing. Carl Swenson, a former teacher at McClymonds High School in Oakland, who was hired to fill the vacancy,[36] was highly competent. However, Nash missed FauntLeRoy greatly.

On the other hand, while he had lost the support of FauntLeRoy, he had apparently regained the patronage of Clark. The reason for Clark's renewed interest in Nash is not immediately apparent, for he continued to complain about his poor financial state which had caused him, among other things, to retire his chief librarian, Robert E. Cowan. Perhaps he felt some guilt in having abandoned an old friend who was financially embarrassed. It seems more likely that he gave Nash some much needed business because of his pride in a Thomas Gray item he had recently acquired from Dr. A. S. W. Rosenbach. It is the only surviving copy of an edition of twelve copies of an ode left unfinished by Gray at the time of his death, which was then completed and published by Gray's literary executor. The *Ode on the Pleasure arising from Vicissitude* appears in the usual Clark Christmas book format; that is, a facsimile printing is accompanied by Nash's own version of the work. It is a small book, comprising less than thirty pages. Even so, the sum which Clark was charged by Nash—$7,500—is a depression price. This item and a strikingly modern Christmas card represent Clark's total commissions for that year.

In 1933 Nash finished the biography of Senator Hearst for William Randolph Hearst. In its technical perfection and its opulent appearance it is a carbon copy of the earlier biography of Phoebe Hearst. Hearst was genuinely pleased with the two books Nash had printed for him and was probably sincere when he said to Nash "of all the pictures, antiques, and other objets d'art I have ever owned— and they have been many and costly—these two books have given me the greatest joy."[37] At the same time, Nash surmised correctly that Hearst's interest would stop with expressions of appreciation. While the two men, who were about equally discomforted by the Depression, remained good friends—the Nashes journeying, for example, to San Simeon on May 1, 1933 to help Hearst celebrate his seventieth birthday—Nash understood clearly that his future association with Hearst would be all pleasure and no business.

In 1933 the Book Club of California gave Nash no business and little occasion for pleasure. Its reluctance, in its currently apprehensive mood, to assume the responsibility for the publication of the second edition of Robert E. Cowan's bibliography of California did place one substantial commission in Nash's hands. He agreed to produce and to publish this important work which, in its second edition, had grown to three volumes. The contract between Nash, Cowan, and Cowan's son shows why Nash agreed to assume the burdensome role of publisher, for it is particularly advantageous to him. The maximum amount of money that Nash was required to pay the compilers, if all 600 sets of the work were sold, was $1,800 or one dollar a volume. Also, Nash was to be reimbursed for all production costs before the first royalties were paid to the Cowans.[38] In this bibliography Nash's typographical talents continued to be apparent. Among the admirers of this work were a reviewer of the *New York Times Book Review*[39] and, locally, the influential Joseph Henry Jackson. Jackson was particularly impressed with the composition of the index which, he observed, "got away entirely from the ordinary matter-of-fact time-table appearance of an index . . . [and which] can stand on the same level as the rest of the letterpress for simple beauty."[40]

Perhaps to buoy up his lagging spirits, Nash issued early in 1934 one of his famous gift items. An attractive printing of Henry W. Longfellow's poem *The Lighthouse*, it is dedicated to President Franklin D. Roosevelt. The colophon states that the broadside was done "to let our great leader know that the major art of printing has recovered." Nash was indulging in some wishful thinking, but the President was sufficiently pleased to respond to Nash's gesture with a gracious letter of acknowledgement which contains a flattering tribute to Nash and to the trade of printing in general. Nash must have shown it with pride to friends and acquaintances and with some relish to those persons who had said that he was finished. The letter was printed in the *San Francisco Call Bulletin*:

24 February 1934

My dear Mr. Nash:

Nothing you could have done would have pleased me as greatly as the copy of "The Lighthouse." If I had not been projected into politics at an early age, I am inclined to believe that I should have sought to be a great printer. "The Lighthouse" is a very beautiful piece of work and will have a special place of honor among my book treasures.

I am grateful to you.

Very Sincerely yours,

s/ Franklin D. Roosevelt.[41]

Nash's new-found optimism must also have impressed the directors of the Zellerbach Paper Company, for that firm asked him, shortly after the appearance of the Longfellow broadside, to produce a contribution to its suspended Keepsake series as a reaffirmation of its faith "in the present and future of our nation."[42] That faith was substantial, judging by the expensive appearance of the item. The Keepsake, devoted to William Caxton, includes a colored reproduction and an account of Caxton's work by Henry L. Bullen.

Nash's health was not equal to his optimism. In one of those unforeseeable setbacks that were to plague his attempts at financial recovery during the Thirties, he suffered in March a physical collapse brought about by overwork that necessitated a long recuperation at a time when he could least afford to be absent from his shop and from San Francisco. Nash had always found travel to be the perfect tonic for his ills; so, at this time, he took a leisurely trip through southern California and Arizona.

While his removal from San Francisco and his shop seems to have been beneficial to Nash's health, there was nothing in the letters he received from Clark to speed his recovery. Again in 1934, in what had become almost an annual ritual, Clark advised Nash that he would not require a Christmas book that year.[43]

Nash had returned to San Francisco in April, and one of the first things he did was to prepare an exhibit in his library of the books he had produced for Clark. His reasons for so doing are obvious. While Clark indicated an interest in the exhibit, he did not attend nor did he send anyone from his staff to represent him. His sudden death at the age of fifty-seven, following a heart attack on June 14 in Montana, terminated the support of Nash's most important patron at the time that he most needed it.

The descending spiral of Nash's affairs which had been accelerated by his own illness and Clark's death was reversed somewhat in the spring and summer of 1934. In May, Nash was made an honorary member of the American Institute of Architects. In July, the Book Club of California asked him to prepare an enlarged edition of Bret Harte's perennially popular *Heathen Chinee*.[44] He did, and the book was selected as one of the Fifty Books of the Year by AIGA.[45] Shortly thereafter, a commission came from the Limited Editions Club of New York City for an edition of Ralph Waldo Emerson's

Essays. Nash's version of this American classic was also selected as one of the Fifty Books of the Year,[46] and its publication was reported in headlines in the December 6 *San Francisco Examiner.* Depression or no, Nash could still make news.

A more striking emergence of the old patterns of Nash's career also occurred that year when Nash was approached by Milton Ray, a local businessman and author whom Nash did not know at the time, who asked him to print a collection of his poetry. Having found in the past that poets and poverty were usually synonymous terms, Nash attempted to make short work of this intruder by announcing that such an undertaking would cost at least $10,000. An exception to Nash's rule, the wealthy Ray quickly agreed to the amount.[47] His commission must have represented for Nash a delightful evocation of the spirit of the deceased Twenties. Nash rewarded this welcome specter with an elegantly printed and bound edition in two volumes of his poems entitled *The Farallones, The Painted World and other Poems of California.*

In 1935, the quantity of Nash's work declined appreciably. Its quality, however, was rigorously maintained. Nash was again represented on AIGA's list of the Fifty Books of the Year for his printing of *Prentice Mulford's California Sketches,*[48] a work done attractively for the Book Club of California. His printing of Catherine C. Phillips' biography of Jessie B. Fremont was a worthy companion to her *Portsmouth Plaza.* The remainder of his publications that year are relatively insignificant.

To compensate for the decline of activity in his printing shop Nash increased the number of exhibits held in his library. In June of 1935, Nash exhibited Templeton Crocker's impressive collection of books from the Aldine Press, all of which were said to be in excellent condition and several of which were in their original bindings. In September, an exhibit of the publications of the Book Club of California was held, and the following month Nash proudly displayed Dr. Otto Vollbehr's incomparable collection of Americana Vetustissima. For each of these exhibits, Nash prepared an attractive catalogue.

In September, Nash was accorded a high honor by Alpha Phi Gamma, the national honorary journalistic fraternity, which had already made him an honorary member in 1932, when that organization proposed to establish a journalistic scholarship in Nash's name at San Francisco State College. To raise the necessary funds, a bridge tournament was held on September 28. Among the sponsors of the event were the Governor of California, the Mayor of San Francisco, the Presidents of the University of California and Mills College, and several of San Francisco's financial and social leaders. One hundred and fifty guests attended, and sufficient funds were raised to establish this scholarship.[49]

However, for every honor there seemed to be a disaster. Nash's expensive Berkeley home was seriously damaged by fire on July 19. Destroyed in the fire were several valuable paintings, some expensive furniture, and the great carved door that Clark had given him.[50] Nash's losses were only partially covered by insurance. He sold the house in 1936.[51]

In poor health and lagging spirits, Nash decided to retire in 1936. He was now sixty-five years old and had been a printer for nearly half a century. On April 21, he announced his decision to the International News Service.[52] A little later, he set the date of his retirement at June 1.[53] Letters and telegrams of felicitation began to pour in. The Book Club of California, whom Nash had served well and generously, sent him its collective good wishes. The San Francisco Club of Printing House Craftsmen, which he had enthusiastically encouraged, held a dinner in his honor on May 21. Encomiums were numerous and sincere. Rumor had it that Nash would be appointed a consultant in typography to the University of California and that he would sell his library to that institution.[54] It was generally agreed that a long and distinguished career had come to a satisfying close.

Only six months later, Nash announced at a luncheon given in his honor at the Biltmore Hotel in Los Angeles by several local printers that his career had resumed and that he would reopen his business as soon as he had returned to San Francisco.[55] Shortly after making this statement, he issued a formal announcement, printed appropriately in the grandiose Nash fashion. The reason he gave for changing his mind was the remarkable recovery of his health: "Now the gift of good health has been restored to me," he states in his announcement, "and I want to work."[56] Other reasons suggest themselves. First, the association of Nash with the University of California proved to be just a rumor. Second, Nash did not really want to retire. Third, it is possible he could not afford to retire. That austere economy *was* essential when he resumed his business is apparent, for Nash placed his beloved library in storage, leasing the space to a commercial printing firm.

Nash stated that this action, which released him from the executive and financial obligations of servicing and maintaining his library, was made so that he should be free to carry out ambitious printing projects.[57] Only one such project was produced in 1936, but it again placed a Nash imprint in the hands of several hundred people. In the winter of that year the Limited Editions Club of New York City published his edition of John Milton's *Paradise Lost* and *Paradise Regained*. The typographical design of this work is unusually austere; it reflected accurately Nash's state of mind.

The ambitious printing projects to which Nash alluded in 1936 never materialized, at least not in comparison to his past achievements. His only substantial publications of 1937 were the bibliography of his imprints produced since 1916—this was compiled by Nell O'Day, Nash's Librarian without a library—and two volumes of Californiana. The bibliography is an elaborate affair, although it is far from being exhaustive. The occasion for the publication of this work was particularly appropriate, for Nash had just completed twenty years as an independent printer. Another publication of 1937, which is in the spirit of Nash's works of the past produced "for the Joy of Doing," was the annual yearbook for the students of Sonora Union High School. The students could not have paid Nash very much for his labor; this fact may have had something to do with their description of Nash as a "humble, sweet, generous, and considerate man."[58] Probably for his more professional attributes Nash was asked by the Book Club of California to produce an edition of Charles C. Dobie's *The Crystal Ball*, the third pamphlet in its series on Contemporary California Short Stories. The Club's state of health had improved decidedly by this time. Membership was back to 500 and seemed capable of even further expansion.[59] That the Club should order 650 copies of the Dobie work from Nash is a clear indication of its renewed confidence in the times and in itself.

The most interesting of Nash's publications after he resumed his business in October of 1936, are three books of Californiana, prepared with the assistance of Herbert Ingram Priestly, the Librarian of the Bancroft Library of the University of California. The series is interesting for three reasons. First, Nash used linotype for its composition. Second, in producing these works Nash acknowledged for the first time the fact that a book's subject might appeal to the collector as much as its imprint. Third, these books are modestly priced. In making the latter two compromises, Nash may have been influenced in part by the success of the Grabhorn brothers' Americana series. Whatever their causes, Nash's compromises were probably too little and too late. The fact that he was willing to try at all is remarkable.

Nash's advertisements for these books show his new orientation: "It is my privilege to announce the publication of a series of three books dealing with California history which should have an irresistible appeal to all collectors of Californiana. I believe that no items of similar interest and rarity have been offered for many years."[60] The three books appeared in close succession. First was John Bidwell's *A Journey to California*, priced at a modest $3.50. This work was followed by Alexander Forbes' *California: a History of Upper and Lower California*, and Guillermo Prieto's *San Francisco in the Seventies*. The latter two books were more expensive than the first but included illustrative matter. Six hundred copies of each of the three books were printed. The series was a financial and critical success. At the time of the appearance of the Prieto work, in January of 1938, Nash reported that only twenty copies of the Bidwell title remained unsold.[61] A further indication of the favorable reception of the entire series was the publication, shortly after the appearance of the Prieto book, of another item of Californiana. This work, a translation by Herbert Ingram Priestly, is entitled *Exposition Addressed to the Chamber of Deputies of the Congress of Union . . . on the Pious Fund* by Don Carlos Antonio Carrillo, and was printed in an edition of 650 copies.

Following these minor triumphs of 1937 and 1938, Nash closed his San Francisco shop permanently. His adjustments to the Depression may have come too late, or he may have decided that he preferred not to continue to make such adjustments. He was not retiring from printing, however, but from San Francisco and from California. The final chapter in his amazing career was to take place in Oregon.

Chapter VI

OREGON

THE MOTIVES which caused Nash to uproot his business and his home from the location where they had thrived for so many years were his desire to preserve his library and his need to sustain his pride. He did not move to Oregon primarily for financial reasons, for by 1938, his business had improved. Besides, Oregon could not at the time offer him a salary. It did offer attractive quarters for his library, an appreciative audience for his work, and the patronage which, if slight compared to that he had enjoyed during the Twenties, so appealed to him. These expectations made Nash an emigrant at the age of sixty-seven.

California had proved to be unworthy of his solicitude. Indeed, it seemed indifferent to it. Nash's greatest dream, after that of printing a Vulgate Bible, was to build in the Bay Area a Palace of Printing Art to contain his library. He had hoped to realize this dream by his sixtieth birthday and did so, in part, when his Berkeley home was completed in 1931. The dream stopped there, for his ultimate plan—to turn his home into a museum which he would then bequeath in perpetuity to the University of California[1]—was not realized. The Depression proved to be stronger than his dream. Nash was in no position in the Thirties to give away the greater part of his wealth, and the University of California was equally unable to recompense him for it. Anxious to retire by 1935, or at least to free himself of the burden of maintaining his valuable library, Nash had offered to sell his collection to the University. It was interested, but Nash was advised at the same time that only funds from private sources could possibly be used for such a purchase. None were forthcoming. Furthermore, Nash was not hired as a typographical consultant to the University Press, as had been rumored. Impulsive as ever, Nash had transformed that bare possibility into an impossibility by announcing in 1936 both the sale of his library and his appointment before either had been agreed to by the University,[2] which was then placed in the awkward position of having to make a public denial.[3] When, the following year, the University commissioned Frederic W. Goudy, a man whom Nash regarded as one of his greatest antagonists, to design a special typeface for the University Press, the insult must have seemed to Nash to have been publicly compounded. The University of California, obviously, could not be counted upon for support or even for sympathy.

Thus, having announced in April, 1936, in expectation of a favorable agreement with the University, that he would shortly retire, Nash was compelled a few months later to announce that he would not retire. A miraculous recovery of his health was given as the reason for his change of mind. His beloved library was placed in storage, and he continued to operate his printing shop while awaiting the appearance of a solution similar to that which the University of California had been unable to provide; but no other local sources came forth with offers. California and, in particular, the Bay Area had disappointed Nash, and their seeming ingratitude hurt him deeply.

Oregon offered a pleasant contrast. There Nash had continued to be appreciated, honored, and lionized since his first public appearance in the spring of 1925 when he spoke at Eugene before the annual convention of Oregon's newspaper editors. He made a profound impact upon that audience which consisted mostly of small-town commercial printers and newspaper editors. Armed with examples of fine printing, from Gutenberg to Nash, which he allowed the audience to handle, Nash forced a confrontation between these men and the heritage of their craft which moved them more than they may have thought possible.

At the University of Oregon, also in Eugene, Nash found an equally appreciative hearing from members of the faculty and the staffs of the library and the University Press, in particular Dean Eric W. Allen of the School of Journalism and Robert C. Hall, the Superintendent of the Press. Dean Allen had been a pioneer in establishing high standards in bookmaking in Oregon. He began in 1917 by opening a press which used as its quarters an abandoned newspaper plant placed at his disposal by its owner. With the addition of Hall to the staff in 1918, the press soon became the University Press, which in a short time earned a reputation for producing attractive printing.[4]

Dean Allen was also responsible for developing at Eugene an excellent School of Journalism which offered its students instruction not only in writing but also in the theory and practice of printing. Because the University Press was under the jurisdiction of the School of Journalism, this alliance was natural and effective. That Nash's audience in 1925 seemed so appreciative was, perhaps, as much the result of Allen and Hall's work as of Nash's performance.

At that first meeting in 1925, everyone seemed to be delighted with Nash, which pleased him greatly. When, during a tour of the Architecture and Allied Arts Department of the University on that same visit, Nash professed to have discovered a genius among the students,[5] his audience became statewide. To help this genius and the other students of the Architecture Department, which he characterized as one of the best in the country, Nash donated $75 towards the purchase of an etching press; etching was the medium of his genius. Nash's reward for having recognized so much talent in Oregon as well as for having made such a good general impression, was a degree of Doctor of Letters conferred upon him by the University of Oregon at commencement exercises held only a few months after his visit. The master salesman had carved out for himself a rich new territory. He was to exploit it fully in the years to come.

Nash was invited to speak again the following year before the Oregon newspaper editors. As a reward for his second appearance, he was voted a life membership in that organization. Moved by this further expression of gratitude, he announced at this meeting that he would like to see a fine arts press established at the University where at least one really fine book would be printed each year, a book whose quality would put the University Press on a par with the presses of Oxford and Cambridge. He calculated that about $1,000 would be needed to purchase additional necessary equipment. If that amount were raised, he offered for his part to come to Oregon to supervise the printing of the fine book and to supply the paper without charge. The alacrity with which his suggestion was accepted may have surprised even Nash, for the assembled newspapermen collected $625 of the specified amount that same day and pledged themselves as well to obtain the balance as soon as possible.[6]

Within a few days of this event, the University made its donation to the cause; Nash was appointed Lecturer in Typography and the History of Printing in the School of Journalism.[7] His duties were to spend ten days to two weeks each year in Eugene, supervising, for the selected book, the designing and composition which were to be done by students. Special rooms for equipment and an office for Nash were allotted to the project in the quarters of the University Press. Dean Allen visited the East during the 1926 Christmas holidays where he was able to obtain a gift from ATF of five hundred pounds of Cloister Light Face type and one hundred pounds of Cloister Italic type.[8] By the first months of 1927, the shop contained most of the equipment requested by Nash.

The year 1927 was anticipated with interest by those persons in Oregon who hoped Nash would help put their state on the typographical map. The newspaper publishers, who had so generously and enthusiastically supported the project, saw another and perhaps more selfish advantage—the availability for employment in Oregon of graduates from the School of Journalism who could claim to have been trained by "the greatest of living printers."[9]

Preparatory to Nash's first official visit to the Eugene campus in his new capacity, the School of Journalism added to its curriculum in the school year 1926–1927 a course in advanced typography. Five students enrolled in this class, and, under the supervision of Robert C. Hall, they produced as a trial run for the first Fine Arts Press book an attractive printing of *Beautiful Willamette*, a poem by the Oregon author Samuel L. Simpson.[10]

Nash selected as the first book of the series an unpublished manuscript entitled *Education and the State* by the late President of the University, Prince L. Campbell. In the design of this the first of the John Henry Nash Fine Arts Press books, the Nash hallmarks are applied with a heavy hand. Hand-set type, handmade paper, Nash's favorite typeface, and a costly binding present a setting that seems to smother the work itself. Nash professed to be delighted with the results, and he stated that this book would certainly "win high opinions for the school forever."[11] Forever is a long time, but Nash's claim was not without some substance. The excessive praise which the book received from the Oregon newspapers[12] is to be expected, and even its highly favorable appraisal in the *Pacific Printer and Publisher*[13] might be said to be the result of regional prejudice. However, the selection of the book for inclusion among the twenty-seven American entries exhibited in conjunction with the international typographical conference held in London in 1929[14] gives some credence to Nash's claim. He had, as was expected of him, put Oregon on the typographical map.

The promise of so auspicious a beginning was not immediately realized, for it was not until 1930 that the second book in the series appeared, and Nash's contributions to its production were slight. He had not, in fact, been able to return to Oregon at all until 1930. The causes for his protracted absence were found in San Francisco. During the years 1928 and 1929, he was immersed in producing three of his most ambitious works—the *Divine Comedy*, *The Life and Personality of Phoebe Apperson Hearst*, and John Dryden's *All for Love*. Also during these years he made two trips to Europe. There was simply no time for him to indulge himself in his Oregon adventure.

The Depression provided him with more time, and one result was a revitalization of the John Henry Nash Fine Arts Press series. It can be said of all these books that they are skillfully produced and interesting. As the work, in part, of students, they attained justified attention and praise, which came occasionally from important quarters. For example, *The Book of Ruth* (1931) and Cobden-Sanderson's *The Ideal Book* (1933) received praise from the *Saturday Review of Literature*,[15] while the *Inland Printer* said of the latter book that it was one of the finest of the several keepsake editions of Cobden-Sanderson's credo.[16] The 1937 edition of Ralph Waldo Emerson's *Compensation* was described by the *Pacific Printer and Publisher* as an exceptionally well-done piece of work.[17] That praise included the presswork which was solely the responsibility of Robert C. Hall and the University Press. Nash continued to be fortunate in the competence of the men who did his presswork.

The series became more regular and its titles more numerous with the removal to Eugene in 1938 first of Nash's library, then his shop, and finally Nash himself. The reasons why Nash was willing to leave San Francisco have been indicated. One of the reasons for his move to Oregon, the warm reception he had received there, has also been noted. More important was the fact that the University of Oregon offered his library a home. The invitation came at a perfect time, for a new and impressive library building had only recently been completed. At the dedication ceremony, held in October of 1937, Nash was one of the speakers. Nash was promised a special room in the new building for his collection and received guarantees that it would be properly maintained and serviced. The University was in no better position to buy Nash's library at this time than had been the University of California two years before. It was understood, however, that the University would attempt to purchase the library when it was in a position to do so, at the depressed price of $50,000.[18] In the meantime, the library was to remain on loan. The removal of the library from San Francisco, where it had been acclaimed not so long ago as one of the ornaments of that city, occasioned little comment. Only a few voices of protest were raised and only a few persons seemed to agree with the observation of the *San Francisco News* that "it seems a reflection on the city and state that it should be lost to us."[19]

At its receiving end, Nash's library was greeted with pomp and ceremony. May 3 was set as the date for a double ceremony to celebrate the first anniversary of the new library building and the opening of the Nash room in that building. The public ceremony was preceded by a private luncheon presided over by President Donald M. Erb. Nash was the honored guest. He gave a short talk—it was his humble craftsman speech—which was warmly received. At the public ceremony there was also an appreciative audience. It is quite apparent that the University community was delighted with the presence of Nash's famous library which, in the eyes of the administration and most of the faculty, added appreciably to the prestige of the University. For the slight cost of removing the collection from San Francisco, the University was to enjoy the use and to bask in the glory of one of the world's leading typographical collections. At a time when the standing of a scholarly library was determined in no small measure by the size of its collection of incunabula, the University of Oregon was suddenly advanced, with the addition of the Nash collection, to the dizzying height of first place among academic

libraries in the western United States.[20] As for Nash, he was delighted to see his library on display again.

Nash was never far for long from his library, and because its new
home was Eugene it is not surprising that his new home should also
be Eugene. It is quite possible, in fact, that the University of Oregon
assumed an obligation to assist Nash in resettling in Eugene as part
of the price for the loan of his library. The resettling included the
removal of his printing shop from San Francisco to Eugene, the costs
of which the University was expected to assume. In return, Nash
agreed to place his shop at the disposal of the students who par-
ticipated in the Fine Arts Press projects, giving them access to a
collection of types and ornaments which in its variety and size was
probably unexcelled in the western United States. Nash would also
continue to use his shop for his own printing. University officials
were quite amenable to this understanding, for it was apparent that
the prestige of the John Henry Nash imprint bearing the name
"Eugene" instead of "San Francisco" would be substantial. Additionally, it was also understood that Nash would be expected to pay
standard rates for the work done for him by the University Press.[21]

It is a clear indication of the University's financial plight at the
time that extensive negotiations had to be carried out by the administration in order to secure the funds to pay for the removal of Nash's
shop to Eugene. Typically, Nash could not comprehend or tolerate
the niceties of bureaucratic maneuvers, and he managed to turn negotiations into a nightmare. When he felt that the University was
taking too long to provide the funds for the removal of his shop, he
decided to try to panic the administration. Suddenly, in the midst
of negotiations between the University administration and state
officials, Nash returned to San Francisco where he announced, "I
plan to stay in San Francisco as long as I live."[22] The crisis was eventually resolved, the money became available, and Nash said a little
later with apparent composure, "I am here to stay for good. This
Oregon campus is the best place on earth."[23] One of his first printings
in Eugene, a Christmas greeting, continued the euphoria. Its message
begins: "If there is a pleasanter little city on the Pacific Coast than
Eugene, Oregon, I for one have not discovered it."[24]

Comfortably resettled at Eugene with access to his library and printing shop, Nash was favorably disposed to spend an increased amount of time with the students enrolled in the typography classes and associated with the John Henry Nash Fine Arts Press. Not that he spent all his time with these students. He declined to accept any formal teaching responsibilities at the University; "I want to go fishing when I want to go fishing," he said.[25]

Yet, during his residence there, the number of John Henry Nash Fine Arts Press imprints and the number of students taking part in printing projects did increase. In 1938 five students worked for most of the academic year hand-setting the type for John William Mackail's *William Morris*. The following year, five students did the composition for an edition of George Parker Winship's *William Caxton*, using a recutting in Nash's possession of Caxton's original black letter type. The same year, one student completed *A True Description of All Trades*, while another hand-set a rather immodest tribute to his teacher entitled *John Henry Nash, Printer*.

University officials were impressed with the results of this flurry of activity. Nash's reward, which was announced in January, 1940, was a half-time appointment, with salary, to the position of Professor of Typography for a period of eighteen months. At the same time, it was also announced that the University had taken an option on the purchase of his library.[26] Nash's response to this official token of his acceptance was to maintain the pace set for the John Henry Nash Fine Arts Press in 1939. In addition to a reprinting of Edward F. O'Day's *Claude Garamond and His Place in the Renaissance*, four shorter works were also printed that year. While the years 1941 and 1942 witnessed a sharp decline in the number of publications and students enrolled in the typography classes, the quality of the work was maintained. For example, *The Sermon on the Mount* (1941) received warm praise from the *Inland Printer*, which said of the composition that the spacing between the words was as nearly perfect as possible.[27] The events of the year 1942, which saw the involvement of the United States in World War II, the continued decline in Nash's state of health, and perhaps a diminishing of the University's interest in Nash's library, contributed to the attrition which soon caused the demise of the John Henry Nash Fine Arts Press. Its final publication, dated 1942, is President Erb's *A Lesson in Courage.* It is typical of Nash's professional integrity that the technical aspects of this final item from the press are of the highest quality.

Between the years 1927 and 1942, the names of sixty-five students appear in the imprints of the John Henry Nash Fine Arts Press books. One of these students, Ray Nash, is a distinguished scholar of the history of printing, now teaching at Dartmouth College. Others assumed important positions with Oregon printing firms and newspapers. For many, however, training and experience, if not interest, ended where they began with one or two classes in typography and some supervised work in composition. Of those who did go on to contribute to the quality of printing in Oregon and elsewhere, it is doubtful that their brief contact with Nash resulted in their obtaining from his instruction any unusual technical or artistic skills. If they had these attributes when they left the University of Oregon, the reasons are to be found more in their own ability and the sound instruction which they received from the regular faculty and staff. However, if the inspiration of example could be measured, who can say that John Henry Nash's contributions to better printing in Oregon were not substantial?

If the University's officials were primarily concerned about the prestige which Nash's presence brought to their campus, they doubtless saw it more in terms of the national reception which his own work continued to receive rather than that accorded to the John Henry Nash Fine Arts Press. Nash's imprints continued to be appreciated by a substantial and widespread audience. These works were few in number, even during his first years in Eugene, and became fewer each year. The cause of this decline was not a lack of consumers. Nash was an elderly man, celebrating his seventieth birthday in 1941, and his health was poor. He, if not the University, regarded his position there as definitely a part-time appointment.

This attitude was, at first, not so apparent, and one of the first items Nash printed at Eugene was an announcement, dated 1939, that he was still in business and still welcomed enquiries. His first book to bear the imprint "Eugene," which was also Nash's most ambitious project there, is an edition of Sir Thomas Browne's *Religio Medici*, printed for the Limited Editions Club. Hard at work on this volume the first month he moved to Eugene, Nash claims to have set the type entirely by hand. He used his favorite Cloister Light Face type, Broadcaster text-paper, and a cover paper imported originally from Germany. This work was well received by the critics, few of whom missed the opportunity its appearance afforded to identify Eugene as "a new focal point for true booklovers,"[28] and the University as "one of the centers of the world's finest book printing."[29]

Published in the first months of 1939, *Religio Medici* was the only book printed by Nash in Eugene which had sufficient distribution to obtain for the University of Oregon a widespread reputation as a center of fine printing. Except for Isaac Cox's *The Annals of Trinity County*, which was published in Oakland by the bookseller Harold C. Holmes in a fairly large edition, most of Nash's works were printed in small editions for private distribution by old friends. For the Cox book, published in 1940, Nash used linotype composition. No stronger evidence of his poor state of health can be imagined.

The last works produced by Nash in Oregon which bear his imprint appeared in 1942. With that year, the romance between the University and Nash came to an end. The University declined to take up its option to purchase his library, and Nash was transferred in June, 1943, to the status of Lecturer Emeritus of Typography.

Nash's seeming new Utopia had disintegrated. In November, he closed his shop, selling some of his equipment and shipping the remainder to Berkeley. Among the purchasers were Harold Seeger, Lawton Kennedy and the Grabhorns, who bought over five hundred pounds of his Inkunabula type eventually used in their printing of Shakespeare's *The Tempest*.[30] His library did not remain in Eugene much longer, finding a permanent home in a few months in the library of the University of California at Berkeley. With the removal from Eugene of Nash, his shop, and his library, the John Henry Nash Fine Arts Press soon expired. Yet Nash left a strong impress upon the tradition of good printing which still exists in Oregon.

Chapter VII
FINAL YEARS

NASH AND HIS WIFE returned to Berkeley in November or December of 1943, establishing their residence in the home of their daughter Mrs. Weldon C. Nichols and her family.[1] As Nash's health permitted, he would visit old friends. He spent much time at Alfred B. and Lawton Kennedy's Westgate Press in Oakland where he was always welcome and where he would occasionally set some type. The Westgate Press still possesses the form which Nash set in the summer of 1946. It consists of eight lines to which has been added this final line: "Last type set by John Henry Nash, August 2, 1946." This statement is not correct, however, for Nash was commissioned by Stanley Marcus, the President of Nieman-Marcus of Dallas, Texas, to prepare a reprinting of his *BeneDictum, Benedicte* for the 1946 Christmas season.[2]

Age had mellowed Nash. He could look back upon a full life and a distinguished career with pride and satisfaction. He tried to settle old enmities which had left scars in his career, and he initiated reconciliations with John Howell, Paul Elder, and Edward DeWitt Taylor. Henry H. Taylor was dead, but perhaps Nash tried to think more kindly of the man than he had in the past.

Even the University of California contributed to this era of good feeling, for in 1944, Nash's library was deposited with that institution. The actual money to purchase the collection, however, came from private funds. The family of Milton Ray—the wealthy poet whose appearance in Nash's shop in the bleak year of 1934 had resulted in so much pleasure and profit for Nash—and a fund established in the name of Albert Bender—the generous ally of so many Bay Area artists—provided the $100,000 which Nash received.[3]

Nash died at his home on May 24, 1947, at the age of seventy-six. The cause of death was arteriosclerosis, a disease from which he had suffered for several years. The Episcopalian recipient of an apostolic blessing was buried at services conducted by the Charter Rock Lodge of the Masonic Order to which he had belonged for several years. Eulogies were numerous.[4]

Chapter VIII
AN APPRAISAL

CARL P. ROLLINS' somewhat carping criticism of Nash's printing of the *Divine Comedy*, described on page 53, evoked from Henry L. Bullen the startling statement that Nash was "America's greatest master of the typographic art."[1] We honor the sound careers of both Rollins and Bullen. Yet, in appraising Nash, they seem to be referring to two very different men. Rollins and Bullen can be said to represent two opinions of Nash which have been in conflict for over half a century. Does one view reflect a decided lapse of judgment, or are both views partly right and partly wrong? It has been one of the purposes of this book, and it is the particular charge of this chapter, to attempt to answer this question and, in so doing, to present an appraisal or, more precisely, a reappraisal of the career of the remarkable John Henry Nash.

In his career Nash played the roles of technician, artist, salesman, and educator. His contemporaries, with some notable and occasionally noisy exceptions that included, in addition to Rollins, Daniel Berkeley Updike, Frederic W. Goudy, Edward DeWitt Taylor, and Henry H. Taylor, rated Nash's performance in all these roles highly. However, in the twenty years following his death, only Nash's reputation as a technician has remained intact. His important role as an educator has been all but forgotten. Posterity, in general, has agreed with Rollins' reservation about Nash as an artist and a salesman. The result has been a total discrediting of Nash's reputation, which is now at its nadir.

Some of the criticisms of Nash's work made by his contemporaries and by subsequent commentators are just criticisms; some seem not to be so. For the latter, two reasons may be suggested. First, some recent critics have judged Nash solely by prevailing standards of fine printing, ignoring the historical fact that such standards are subject to change. To evaluate any printer completely outside his setting is to do him an injustice. Second, and in general, critics have not bothered to ascertain what Nash was trying to do and then to determine how well he achieved his goal. A judicious critic might want at least to consider the proposition that a fine printer should be evaluated as much for how effectively he accomplished what he set out to do as for that critic's opinion of the value of his aims. Few of Nash's critics have done so.

Nash is probably not "America's greatest master of the typographic art," but neither is he the incompetent suggested by Rollins. What he really is will be described in this chapter under the following rubrics: Nash the technician, the artist, the salesman, and the educator.

TECHNICIAN

Nash's severest critics have acknowledged his exceptional performance as a technician. In the standards he maintained in composition, presswork, binding, and quality of material, Nash was the complete perfectionist. He could not abide inferior material or the indifferent handling of good material, and he established a level of printing and bookmaking few other modern printers have equalled.

Nash's perfection is even more impressive because it is present in so much of his work. His insistence upon the perfect handling of the best material was not applied selectively. The vast majority of the hundreds of items, from elaborate books and broadsides to calling-cards and envelopes, which his San Francisco shop produced from 1916 to 1938 and which he issued from his Eugene shop between 1938 and 1942, reflect his unwavering application of high standards. Only towards the end of his long career do we find examples of relatively inferior bookmaking. The quality of Nash's work before 1916 is also uneven for the good reason that he was required to use the material and the staff supplied by his various employers. Even under these conditions, however, while the material, presswork, and binding are occasionally inferior, the composition is seldom so and that identified by Nash as specifically his work is exceptionally good. During his brief tenure with the Sunset Press and the Twentieth Century Press, in both of which firms he was a part owner, Nash began in a modest way to apply his high standards to material, presswork, and binding as well as to composition. His work for the Tomoyé Press and Paul Elder and Company shows great technical ingenuity and, considering the limitations of time and money, presents surprisingly numerous examples of fine printing. The material, on the other hand, is not always of the best quality. Taylor, Nash & Taylor and Blair-Murdock enabled Nash to apply his standards to every aspect of bookmaking but within set financial limitations. Throughout Nash's association with these several firms, from 1901 to 1916, the corpus of his work presents clear evidence of his *desire* to achieve perfection. That he was not always able to do so was not his fault nor, considering their purpose, that of the people for whom he worked. There was simply no demand for the best printing of which Nash and probably several of his associates were capable.

Once he had established his own firm in 1916, Nash literally created a demand, and this may be his most important contribution to the development of fine printing in San Francisco. Among Nash's predecessors in San Francisco were men whose skill and enthusiasm equalled and whose artistry often exceeded his, but their potential was never fully realized because the market was not available to encourage it. Nash's ability to develop new audiences for fine printing, which these men lacked, supplied the market. Additionally, because he was able to command the highest prices for his work from that market, Nash could express fully his goals. At the height of his career Nash marshalled the best material and talent available from the Orient, Europe, and the United States. The results of this unprecedented enterprise were to win for him an international reputation as one of the greatest technicians of the printing trade. His success in creating what was said to be the perfection of printing impressed his contemporaries profoundly. It has left many of us indifferent perhaps because we, unlike they, cannot appreciate the excitement caused by the experiment itself. Nor can we, unlike they, agree with Nash that in achieving technical perfection he had also achieved artistic perfection.

Nevertheless, Nash the technician is still regarded as the ideal in fine printing circles, particularly those on the West Coast, and his influence in this role continues to be felt. One San Francisco fine printer, in complaining recently that it was not possible to get the kind of printing desired from a cylinder press added, "although they say John Henry Nash did."[2] Another local printer, whose style is almost totally antipathetic to Nash's and whose reputation is as high now as Nash's was in the Twenties, admits that Nash's work was amazingly well done.[3] A third San Francisco fine printer, who is equally renowned as a book designer, makes this appraisal of Nash's contributions: "Nash's impact on San Francisco printing still persists in the perfection of craftsmanship, the attention to spacing, and the incredibly good presswork he exacted from his collaborators."[4]

Nine years ago, George Macy, the President of the Limited Editions Club, for whom Nash had printed four books, observed in retrospect that technically each of Nash's books was near perfection.[5] At an earlier period, Macy's praise of Nash's work was less qualified. He said, for example, of Benjamin Franklin's *Autobiography* (1931) that "it is our profound conviction . . . that this book is the finest instance of book making which we have yet sent to our members."[6] Three years later, in reference to Nash's edition of Ralph Waldo Emerson's *Essays* (1934), Macy said that "there is no printer who excels Mr. Nash in the craftsmanlike meticulousness of his book printing."[7] In announcing to club members the impending publication of John Milton's *Paradise Lost* and *Paradise Regained* (1936), Macy's praise reached its peak. Nash, he said, was doing the best printing ever achieved in America.[8] It is the highest compliment to Nash that it is not easy to think of another American printer about whom this statement seems more valid, if "best printing" be understood to refer to technical considerations.

ARTIST

Stanley Morison has stated that the essentials of fine printing are care and intelligence.[9] Nash's care has never been in question; it was extraordinary. His intelligence—and by this word I understand Mr. Morison to mean that combination of knowledge, imagination, and sure taste which, along with care, may create fine printing—has not always enjoyed so high an opinion in the minds of his critics. While care in fine printing is an absolute quality which can be determined outside considerations of prevailing times and changing tastes, any evaluation of a printer's intelligence must be influenced by both. What some of Nash's recent critics have neglected is the responsibility to consider two times and tastes—the printer's as well as their own.

Even a cursory investigation of Nash's period clearly discloses the allusive and imitative character of typography which then prevailed. ATF, Monotype, and other typefoundries were manufacturing a wide variety of typefaces based upon historical models. These were eagerly accepted by printers, if not always aptly applied, and their use stimulated an interest as well in the history of printing and historical typography. The period was "backward-harking"[10] and eclectic, and Nash's style fitted naturally and comfortably into it. While a different backward-harking and eclectic style developed by Nash's New England colleagues, which produced "a demure, practical English Old-style book,"[11] happens to be in favor today, it should be remembered that Nash's style was in general harmony with its time and in particular accord with its place, for the grand manner of bookmaking reigned in California. To judge his style completely by today's preferences is to deny the important consideration of historical context.

Nash's style encompassed several styles. With occasional borrowings from certain eighteenth-century English printers, the Chiswick Press, the Kelmscott Press, the Doves Press, and in the United States the work of Theodore Low DeVinne, and Bruce Rogers, his style focused primarily upon the printers of the incunabula period and the following century. Erhard Ratdolt and Nicolas Jenson were his particular favorites, and many of Nash's typographic pictures are modeled upon their work. He preferred their printing because he felt an affinity for their styles, but he also looked upon it as representing the perfection of craftsmanship. Hence, in his own work, his obsession with perfect printing and bookmaking and his rejection of the mechanical for the hand-produced. Nash saw his typographical pictures primarily in terms of these factors.

While Nash's care is equal and in certain respects superior to that of his models, because of mechanical improvements in printing, his intelligence is not, a fact which is even more apparent when the latter is contrasted to his own superlative care. Individual items among Nash's work—for example, those identified by Joseph Faunt-LeRoy in his biography of Nash and cited earlier in this study—

show knowledge, imagination, and taste, but they are exceptions to a rule which, while displaying an impressive array of formats, material, typefaces, and ornaments, presents at the same time a series of rigid variations on two or three archaic typographical themes.

One effect of this rigidity is inappropriate design. Nash was not obviously influenced by subject matter in his choice of design because he either could or would not establish any correlation between the two. One result of this weakness, according to George Macy, was that Nash was frequently unable to convey the spirit of a book to the reader.[12] Style to Nash became increasingly monumental; he would have only a city of palaces. While not unsuited to such works as the *Divine Comedy* and the *Psalms of the Singer David*, Nash's style seems distorted and occasionally ludicrous when applied to much of the material he printed including, for example, an announcement of a local furrier's line, a volume of mediocre poetry, the biography of an undistinguished person, and even to any workaday book that was written to be read. In reviewing an example of the latter category, Nash's printing of Catherine Phillips' *Portsmouth Plaza* (1932), Carl Rollins asked and answered the pertinent question: "When is a book not a book?" "A book is not a book when you cannot see the text for the technique."[13] His point is well taken. It is perhaps even more forcefully made by Edwin Grabhorn: "Nothing on a page should pop when you are reading it."[14]

Nash's own goals, which incidentally were not Rollins' or Edwin Grabhorn's, tend to mitigate these criticisms somewhat. Nash saw the physical printed item, regardless of the significance or subject of its text, as a work of art completely equal to painting, sculpture, and architecture.[15] He concluded correctly, as his success must indicate, that his clients thought likewise. "The people who bought my edition did so because they knew it was beautifully printed," he wrote in a letter in reference to his *Divine Comedy*. "Practically all of my purchasers are collectors of fine printing, and are particularly interested in books from that angle."[16] And if, as George Macy states, Nash's ability to convey the spirit of the book was wanting, these clients, including many members of Macy's own

Limited Editions Club, were as unaware of this flaw as was Nash.

In censuring Nash's artistry, we are in effect rejecting the popular concept of fine printing which prevailed during much of his career. Time and experience have probably made us more sophisticated connoisseurs of the book beautiful than they, in the respect that we do not necessarily equate fine printing with large format, hand production using handmade material, and an elaborate style. We look today at the best-known of Nash's work—the *Life of Dante*, the *Divine Comedy*, the Hearst biographies, and the series of Clark books—and are still impressed with individual details in their production, including the beauty of the paper and binding, the careful composition and presswork, and the frequently effective combinations of paper, ink, and color. Yet somehow these books seem flat, dull, and, paradoxically considering Nash's aims, a little mechanical. One is reminded in reviewing the body of Nash's printing, which seems to make a sad regression from rigidity to frigidity,[17] of the work of another perfectionist, T. J. Cobden-Sanderson, which is a little automatic and boring. Cobden-Sanderson at least realized the price of his and Nash's kind of perfection. He is said to have told Edward Johnson once that he wished he could place a sign on the door of his shop which read "For God's sake do something careless!"[18] Cobden-Sanderson's comment adds a dimension to his personality which Nash's totally lacks. Nash was incapable of self-doubt.

SALESMAN

A salesman is only as good as his confidence in himself. That same lack of self-criticism which contributed in part to Nash's artistic limitations strengthened the efficacy of his salesmanship. Had Nash not been so good a salesman, his success could not have been so great, for it was based almost entirely upon his ability to sell himself and his product.

In part this ability was accidental; it resulted from the kind of man Nash happened to be. It was also the result in part of an accident of ideal time and place for, as has been mentioned, the prosperous and extravagant Twenties were the heyday of the cult of the salesman and California was a perfect setting for Nash's grand style. Personality, however, was more important to Nash's success than time and place. Nash had had to sell himself initially during the troubled months before the entry of the United States into World War I, and he was to continue to have to sell himself during the Depression of the Thirties. Where other men in good times had achieved modest success, Nash had secured wealth and fame, and where others in bad times had failed, he had persevered.

What kind of salesman was Nash? Above all, he was a consummate showman with a remarkable ability to impress a wide variety of audiences. He has been accurately described as the Barnum of the business.[19] To Nash's largest audience, the general public, he was an interesting and colorful man and a dedicated artist who had fought the good fight for his ideals, had won, and had been handsomely rewarded. He was a perfect Anthony Adverse for the Twenties, and his exploits were widely reported and generally savored. Nash's acting ability in this performance is impressive, for while the general public saw him as a dynamic man, which he was, it also saw this proud, explosive non-intellectual as a person who was modest,[20] imbued with "a sort of Greek serenity,"[21] and a great humanist.[22] In his library, his shop, and the countless places where he made public appearances Nash played all of these roles with relish.

In playing these roles, Nash was quite willing to take his show on the road. Armed with examples of fine printing, including his own, of course, he spoke frequently and effectively about his art to an impressive array of people. In the greater Bay Area alone, the Charter Rock Lodge of the Berkeley Masons, the students of Mills College, members of the Concordia Club, the Palo Alto Art Club, the Club Beaux Arts, the Santa Cruz Rotarians, and the Oakland Forum were among the groups enlightened and entertained by Nash. His itinerary became increasingly ambitious, taking him throughout the remainder of California and into Arizona, Oregon, and Washington. He could secure the most unlikely places as theaters for his performances. We learn, for example, that in May of 1930 an exhibit of fine printing prepared by Nash was proudly displayed in the lobby of the First National Bank in Salem, Oregon.[23]

Another role, that of a man's man, came naturally to Nash and stood him in particular good stead with financiers and businessmen who were his cronies. He was an avid fisher and golfer and an automobile enthusiast. Cadillacs, next to his family and his business, were a chief source of pride and joy, and for several years he was a kind of unofficial ambassador for Don Lee Cadillac of San Francisco. He was completely at ease among businessmen who found in Nash nothing precious, arty, or eccentric. They liked and respected Nash and were numbered among his most loyal clients and patrons. Although not all of them understood Nash's ideas about the book beautiful, they could appreciate and be impressed by his methods of selling. They must certainly have regarded him to be as great a salesman as he was said to be a printer. Indeed, his salesmanship which became a legend, was held up as a model for businessmen in general. In a typical response to Nash's method, the *San Francisco Grocer* urged its subscribers to emulation:

We know of one man who simply began where other printers left off. He threw his whole spirit into the effort to be a different kind of a printer from the others he had met. He kept on striving to attain what he conceived to be the acme of excellence in printing. What is the result? Well there is more difference between John Henry Nash and the average first class printer than there is between the finest grocery store in the land and the corner grocery. . . . Now we haven't written this article to advertise Mr. Nash [although, of course, this is just what they did]. Our thought is to inspire grocers with the idea that they too may strike out upon paths untrodden by others.[24]

The intellectual community was impressed by a different Nash, for it saw him as an artist dedicated to presenting and preserving in what was said to be a masterful and monumental form the works of past and contemporary authors of renown. They thought that Nash's printing was done to display the contents of books, and that his chief end was to "serve literature as reverently as an acolyte on the altar serves God."[25] George Sterling, Edwin Markham, and other local literary luminaries who were flattered by the elegant dress Nash gave their works, looked upon him as a fellow artist. Within the intellectual community, educators were among Nash's strongest advocates. One of his first champions was Dr. Aurelia Reinhardt, the scholarly President of Mills College. Primarily through her efforts and, of course, the effects of his own salesmanship, Nash received formal academic recognition when Mills College bestowed upon him the honorary degree of Master of Arts in 1923. Similar honors followed from the University of Oregon and the University of San Francisco. John Henry Nash became "Dr. John Henry Nash," a signature which he proudly attached to all public communiqués.

To the Roman Catholic and Jewish communities of San Francisco, Nash was a sympathetic and interested friend. In an era not known for its religious tolerance, Nash made public display of his respect for and appreciation of these groups and the support they had given him. His actions were reciprocated by individuals and official bodies, including, in the case of the Roman Catholics, the Vatican itself. Additionally, his style was suited perfectly to their printing needs.

Nash's role as doyen of the printing and publishing community probably received the strongest reaction, which in this case was negative as well as positive. Among those printers who shared Nash's interest in fine printing and the book beautiful were some of his strongest advocates who had been profoundly impressed by Nash's words and deeds. Many of Nash's colleagues, however, because they could not understand his message or objected to it or its form of delivery, constituted Nash's most sceptical audience. These persons found the man and his methods intolerable, a feeling which was no doubt intensified by the degree of his financial and popular success.

At the same time, however, Nash never lacked for local admirers among his associates. "Nash Nights" were a fixture of the printing community's social life during the Twenties and even the less hospitable Thirties. One such event in 1925 may be cited as an example. For it was printed a booklet entitled *A Tribute to John Henry Nash, A.M.* which was signed by nearly every local printer interested in quality bookmaking. The message written in the booklet is Nashian in its style:

> May your artistic ability continue
> Appreciation of your merit increase
> Ourselves long enjoy the pleasure of your society
> and future generations emulate the deeds
> of him we this night meet to honor.

Similar honors, which were also in large part the reward for Nash's salesmanship, were forthcoming from an amazing variety of quarters. A John Henry Nash Room was installed at Occidental College and another at the University of Oregon. In 1929 a Nash

Room was dedicated in the private Los Altos residence of Max M. Cohn, the San Francisco financier. The new building into which Nash moved his business in 1925 was called the John Henry Nash Building, although he was merely one of its several tenants. A John Henry Nash Poetry Prize was established in the Twenties at Mills College. He was given honorary membership in important journalistic and architectural societies. His work was complimented by two Presidents of the United States and by the Pope. It was supported by two of the wealthiest millionaires in an age of millionaires, and these men called Nash their friend as well. Nash so dominated the fine printing movement in San Francisco that one admirer, in a reaction which was not unusual, turned the entire fine printing movement upside down by referring in apparent sincerity to William Morris as a Victorian Nash![26] "All in all," said another enthusiast, "Nash is more than an individual. He is an institution."[27] Above all, the salesman had built the institution.

EDUCATOR

If in retrospect Nash's salesmanship seems somewhat tawdry and his artistry questionable, his role as an educator continues to gain stature. Yet, the spectacular elements of both of the former played an important part in the effectiveness of Nash's performance as an educator, for they enabled him to secure one of the largest and most receptive audiences ever assembled by a fine printer. Of Nash's contemporaries only Elbert Hubbard, another incomparable salesman, was so generally well known, and his influence has not been so long lived.

Nash's success as an educator of the public was important to the fine printing movement in San Francisco, for it helped to create a market for the work of his successors as well. His more direct influence upon printers was even more important to the development there of the quality of fine printing. Printers with aspirations to become fine printers profited most from the examples Nash provided of his financial and popular success and the model of quality printing and bookmaking. He showed them that there was a substantial market for fine printing, where none had existed before, which would pay higher prices than had previously been thought possible. "He set the standard," says Lawton Kennedy, "that when a thing was worth anything, it was worth paying for."[28] He had proven in San Francisco what Elbert Hubbard had shown in East Aurora, that "there is a market for the best, and the surest way . . . to get away from competition is to do your work a little better than the other fellow."[29] Nash's efforts had transformed his printing into an art in the minds of his public, and as a result he was able to enjoy the profits which obtained from one's being able, in the words of Dr. A .S. W. Rosenbach, to price a volume on its worth, not its cost.[30]

Nash's financial and popular success attracted other men interested in producing fine printing in San Francisco. Among the first of these were Haywood H. Hunt and Edwin Grabhorn. Hunt came to San Francisco in 1915 to see the Panama-Pacific International Exposition. He remained to print because he observed that San Francisco was producing the best printing on the West Coast. He was particularly impressed by the amount of book printing that the area was supporting, and he attributes this situation to Nash's "trailblazing."[31] Four years later, Edwin Grabhorn came to San Francisco partly, says his brother Robert, because "he knew Nash was here and there was support for that kind of printing, because Nash was getting it."[32] Other printers, in the following years, would settle in San Francisco for the same reasons.

Nash's work set standards of printing and bookmaking for these same men. Whether they were in sympathy with his style or not, and some never were, the technical quality of Nash's work was a yardstick by which they could compare their own. For some, Nash provided the very necessary element of competition which acted as a tonic and a stimulus and which made the game worth playing. More often, however, Nash's work was something to try to emulate, not to try to excel. The following letter from James Johnson, whose Windsor Press was to become one of San Francisco's best printing shops, reflects this more typical response to Nash's influence:

23 October 1925

Dear Mr. Nash,

You will pardon the liberties I am taking in addressing this letter to you. The fact is that it is something stronger than myself which impels me to write.

Only yesterday by the kind permission of Charles McIntyre, I was privileged to view for the first time, some of your works. It was a revelation. The memory of seeing these works will be with me all of my life and shall be my inspiration. Mr. Nash, if you had created only one book in your span of life and that book was "Ecclesiastes" it alone would acclaim you as the greatest printer of modern ages, for that work is immortal.

I repeat that your work was both a revelation and inspiration to me and shall govern and impel me along the path that leads to the doing of better things for the same love of doing.[33]

Nash's influence spread beyond the boundaries of San Francisco. In Los Angeles the excellent printer Bruce McCallister wrote in 1922 that Nash's work "should be an inspiration to all who use the printed word. His ideals, if only partially adopted, would immeasurably elevate printing."[34] In Haywood H. Hunt's opinion "it would be difficult to estimate the number of budding typographers who owe their start to John Henry Nash who inspired rising printers to improve their style."[35]

Johnson's letter portrays Nash as a rather aloof man and his influence as somewhat remote. Actually, he was directly and frequently in contact with those younger printers whom he felt to be sincere and capable of producing good work. They were always welcome in his shop and library, which they usually left with an armload of examples of his work. However, Nash's interest in fine printing did not stop with his own, and he was generous with his time and counsel to fledgling printers. One such, who is now numbered among California's best printers, wrote this letter of appreciation to Nash for his guidance:

May 9, 1940

Dear Mr. Nash,

I was extremely gratified the other night at Occidental College when I saw you in the audience, and remembered your kindness many years ago when I went to San Francisco to ask you for your advice on becoming a printer. Your generosity with your time on that occasion, when you took me through your shop and showed me the beautiful examples of printing in your library and with good advice encouraged me, has always made me consider you as a godfather of my printing career.

So you can see how happy I was to see you at the talk I gave.

Most sincerely,
s/ Ward Ritchie[36]

The fact that Nash took seriously the responsibilities of his role as educator is seen as clearly in the formation and display of his library as in his personal advice and assistance to individual aspiring fine printers. His library supported his efforts to instruct the printing trade and laymen alike, and its very effective use in this role shows again his remarkable talent for promotion. It also shows his vision, for its creation, let alone its public display, set him far apart from most of his colleagues who found his interest in *collecting* books to be almost incomprehensible. Indeed, when Nash first began purchasing examples of fine printing for his library, his efforts, which were regarded by many of his fellow printers as pretentious and ill advised, were treated with derision. When the news got around that Nash had paid $1,000 for a copy of the Kelmscott *Chaucer*, it is said that shortly thereafter his secretary, Mae Hartmann, was stopped in the street by a printer who generously offered to assist her in finding another position when Nash "blew up, as his foolishness seemed to make certain."[37]

Nash's "foolishness" in this particular case proved to be shrewdness, for the money spent on his Kelmscott *Chaucer* as well as on his entire collection was an excellent financial investment. His general "foolishness" resulted in large measure in the singular success of his entire career. If received with better response it could have contributed even more than it did to the enrichment of San Francisco's printing community. This is another example of Nash's "foolishness": to establish in San Francisco a Graphic Arts Library and Museum which would contain not only Nash's excellent library and shop but also the contents of ATF's library and museum and a papermaking shop and museum. Plans were actually drawn for the building,[38] and if the crash of 1929 had not frightened away a prospective patron and his million dollar gift,[39] it would probably have been built, thanks primarily to Nash's efforts. Following the collapse of the entire project, Nash tried to salvage at least one of its features—the acquisition of the library and museum of ATF. Henry L. Bullen, the person who had built this excellent collection, gave Nash's efforts his enthusiastic support, perhaps in part because he was to have accompanied it to San Francisco to become a kind of scholar in residence. For lack of sufficient local interest, however, Nash had to abandon even this project, this foolishness. ATF's library is now one of the ornaments of the library of Columbia University.

On another occasion this unaccountable interest in libraries on the part of a printer helped to preserve in San Francisco an important collection when, in 1933, the California state legislature was debating whether or not to return the Sutro Library to the Sutro family in order to "save" $4,000 a year in the salaries of two librarians. Nash was outraged. Weighted down at the time with his own financial problems and poor health he could not, nevertheless, tolerate in silence such short-sightedness. His was certainly the most forceful and perhaps the most effective voice raised in protest against this proposal. Under the headline "Nash Attacks Sutro Library Return" the *San Francisco Call Bulletin* printed Nash's scathing open letter to the people of San Francisco. His flattering references to southern California were well calculated to arouse local pride:

As a printer, collector and lover of fine and rare books I voice the opinion of thousands of San Francisco book lovers when I say I was appalled at this announcement. My work as a maker of books has brought me into close contact with many of the founders of great libraries, such as the Morgan, Huntington and Clark collections. I recall very well that many years ago Henry E. Huntington told me he had wished to place his library in San Francisco, but due to trickery of politicians his plan was frustrated. My good friend William Andrews Clark, Jr. of Los Angeles whose collection of English classics is one of the finest in the world, also told me he had wished his library could have been placed in San Francisco. Los Angeles is rich in libraries. The Huntington and Clark libraries alone would place her in an enviable position and only last year the million dollar Doheny Memorial Library was presented to the University of Southern California. San Francisco can boast of no such possessions. Libraries, art galleries and museums are the properties that make cities great and interesting. Instead of striving to save $4,000 a year San Franciscans should be urging the erection of a suitable building to house the Sutro Library, where it might be used for research or pleasure by thousands who are still in ignorance of its existence.

If San Francisco allows the Sutro Library to be returned to the Sutro Family it will be to her everlasting discredit.[40]

The Sutro Library has remained in San Francisco in public ownership.

Nash's solicitude for this library was not totally unselfish, for he had probably already decided to sell his own library and with his usual business acumen realized that to stimulate a public interest in the Sutro Library was to benefit the possible sale of his own. There are elements of self-interest in most of Nash's actions promoting the interests of fine printing, of libraries, and of the other causes he espoused, and his performances in his several roles, including that of educator, were calculated to reflect on the greater glory of John Henry Nash. He was not a modest man; there was little reason for him to be modest. Indeed, had he been so, his career and its salutary effects upon the development of fine printing in San Francisco would probably have been insignificant.

Nash's vision extended far beyond the myopic limits of most of his fellow printers. He saw that there was a market in San Francisco for fine printing, that the market was far larger than had been thought possible, and that it could be secured by a person of determination and enterprise. Nash's remarkable career cultivated in San Francisco an enthusiasm for fine printing which has outlived him, his method, and his style. He will remain controversial, and his reputation will probably continue to experience alternating cycles of praise and censure. The existence and continuation of a fine printing movement in San Francisco will remain a more constant memorial to Nash, for his career is the foundation-stone of that movement.

APPENDIX:
A DESCRIPTION OF THE LIBRARY
AND TYPOGRAPHICAL MUSEUM

NASH's LIBRARY and Typographical Museum was assembled over a long period of time, at first rather haphazardly and later more systematically as Nash evolved in his mind the kind of collection he wanted. His model was ATF's Library and Typographical Museum, which he first saw during his residence in New York City from 1906 to 1909. Following his return to San Francisco, the establishment of his own firm, and the marked improvement in his financial status, Nash became a serious collector. The Twenties, in particular, saw major additions to his collection, the result not only of his augmented income but also his trips to Europe and its bookshops. Even during the Thirties, when Nash's access to bookdealers and to cash was substantially reduced, he continued to purchase items for his library and museum.

The collection finally purchased for the University of California in 1944 was not identical to the one Nash in the late Twenties had envisioned bequeathing to that institution, for the impressive assortment of type and other printing equipment was separated by that time from the main collection and widely scattered. The library, if not the museum, remains intact, consisting of approximately three thousand items about equally divided between Nash's own imprints and those of other individuals and firms. Nash's collection of his own printings is without doubt definitive, for during his independent career he assiduously kept copies of everything that was issued from his shop, including even envelopes, letterheads, and Christmas cards. At the same time his librarian and he also searched in bookshops for copies of those items on which he had worked as a compositor during the years before he established his own firm in 1916.

His collection of the work of other printers is impressive in aggregate, although it is not particularly systematic or well balanced. His holdings of incunabula are disappointing considering his interest in the period, which sometimes bordered on an obsession. For the years 1501 to 1800, Nash's library contains some excellent individual items, but again the collection for this period as for the previous one is not exhaustive, even for individual printers, and it is also not effectively representative. Nash was a more intelligent and confident collector of examples of nineteenth and twentieth century fine printing and typography. His holdings for this period are impressive in their quality and their quantity—about one thousand items.

The museum, a weak copy of ATF's Typographical Museum, is a mixed bag, including some but not all of Nash's business papers, photographs of and mementos from his fellow printers, a type mould, some punches and type, and a rather impressive collection of coins and medals associated with printing and printers.

The purpose of the discussion which follows is to provide a description rather than an inventory of Nash's Library and Typographical Museum. A typed inventory of the entire collection already exists, as well as the original card catalogue of Nash's library. These may be inspected in the Rare Books and Special Collections Room of the University Library of the University of California at Berkeley.

THE LIBRARY

MANUSCRIPTS

Nash's library contains only one manuscript book, a fifteenth-century Italian antiphonal. This and two leaves from liturgical works are the only manuscripts in the collection. Nash, obviously, did not feel secure as a collector of manuscripts, and he had no real interest in them.

PRINTED MATERIAL: INCUNABULA

The earliest example of printing from movable type in Nash's library is a leaf from the 42-line Gutenberg *Bible*. Separate leaves from other early printed works are included, of course, in Nash's copies of Konrad Haebler's editions of German, Italian, and West European incunabula. Still other interesting fragments are eleven leaves from a Latin *Bible* printed by Adolph Rusch for Anton Koberger (1479) and a single leaf from an edition of Augustinus' *Epistolae* printed by Johann Mentelin at Strasbourg, circa 1471.

The prize of the eleven complete incunables, and Nash's own

favorite, is a beautiful copy of *Hypnerotomachia Poliphili* (Venice: Aldus, 1499). Nash took great pride in this copy which is untrimmed and in its original binding. Erhard Ratdolt, who was one of Nash's favorite printers, is represented by five works: the *Calendarium* (Venice, 1476); *De Bella Civilibus* (Venice, 1477) of Appianus; the attractive *Elementa Geometria* of Euclid (Venice, 1482); *Chronicon* of Eusebius (Nash's copy was a gift from Dr. A. S. W. Rosenbach); and *Sermones de Laudibus Sanctorum* by Robertus Caracciolus (Augsburg, 1489). Two incunables of Nicolas Jenson, another printer whose work Nash greatly admired, are included: Augustinus' *De Civilate Dei* (Venice, 1475); and the 1470 Eusebius *De Evangelica Praeparatione*, which first used Jenson's famous roman type. One of Nash's most impressive incunables is a fine copy of a quarto book of hours printed by Philippe Pigouchet in 1498. Its woodcut borders are quite handsome. Nash's incunable collection contains only one example of a *Bible*, the 1476 Venice edition printed by Franciscus Renner, de Heilbronn and Nicolaus de Frankfordia. The *Nuremberg Chronicle* (1493) is represented by a good copy.

PRINTED MATERIAL: 16TH–18TH CENTURIES

In this section are eight titles whose subject pertains to printing and printers. The most famous of these is an excellent copy of Geoffroy Tory's *Champ Fleury* (Paris, 1529) which Nash had bound by the Riviere firm. Other titles in this category are Pieter Schyijver's *Lavre-Crans voor Lavrens Coster van Haerlem* (Haarlem: Adriaen Rooman, 1628); *Manuel Typographique* by Pierre Simon Fournier (Paris: 1764–1766); Joseph Ames' *Typographical Antiquities* (London: W. Faden for J. Robinson, 1749); Philip Luckombe's *The History and Art of Printing* (London: W. Adlard and J. Browne for J. Johnson, 1771); Domenico Maria Manni's *Vita di Aldo Pio Manuzio* (Venice: Giambatista Novelli, 1759); Gerard Meerman's *Origines Typographicae* (The Hague: Nicolaus van Daalen, 1765); and Samuel Palmer's *The General History of Printing* (London: Palmer, 1732).

Seven *Bibles* are represented in this section, two of which are particularly noteworthy: Robert Estienne's 1549 Paris *Bible* and John

Baskerville's 1763 Cambridge *Bible*. Virgil is also represented by seven editions, including two by Baskerville and the famous Aldine 1501 version. Of the latter work, Nash boasted that his copy was the finest in the world in that it is not only in excellent condition but is also an inch larger than other copies.

These important three hundred years in the development of printing are represented by good examples of the work of several fine printers of the period, including, with the number of examples in Nash's collection indicated in parentheses, Aldus (2); Baskerville (3); Bodoni (2); the Clarendon Press (2); the Elzevir family (4); the Estienne family (2); the Foulis Press (3); Froben (2); and one each of Benjamin Franklin, the Giunti family, Joachim Ibarra, Balthazar Moretus, Christopher Plantin, the Sessi family, Peter Shoeffer, and the Strawberry Hill Press.

PRINTED MATERIAL: 19TH–20TH CENTURIES

Works about printing and examples of fine printing of this period form the preponderance of Nash's library. Many of the items in this section were gifts from other printers to Nash. Several of these, because of the inscriptions they carry, have added association value.

In this section, over two hundred and fifty titles deal with the subject of typography. These include facsimile editions of earlier classics, type specimen books, manuals and treatises. The majority of books and ephemera, however, represent examples of fine printing. This section of Nash's library is certainly the most comprehensive and well balanced. It, along with the collection of Nash imprints, is the basis for the real value of the library. The following English presses are particularly well represented: the Chiswick Press (27); the Kelmscott Press (8), including excellent copies of the *Chaucer*, the *Golden Legend*, and the *Story of the Glittering Plain*; the Doves Press (14 items), including the *Bible*; and the Ashendene Press (3). American printers and designers are also well represented. Among these are Theodore Low DeVinne (14); the Merrymount Press (27); Bruce Rogers and Riverside Press imprints (70); and the Limited Editions Club (72). Among the other American printers who are well represented are Edwin Rudge, Hal Marchbanks, the Grabhorn Press, and other less well-known San Francisco printing houses.

THE MUSEUM

As has been stated, the Museum is somewhat disappointing except for the excellent medal and coin collection (see typed inventory for a complete list). Even Nash's business papers are not complete. In particular, the absence of his ledgers and dockets represents a crucial gap. However, his business correspondence is included in the papers housed in the Museum, and this seems to be quite complete. The papers contain as well the copy and proof of several of Nash's publications. A small miscellany of memorabilia rounds out the museum collection. The following description is divided into three sections: business papers; copy, proof, and related letters; miscellaneous.

BUSINESS PAPERS

Aside from copies of a few bills, Nash's business papers consist entirely of correspondence. Arranged alphabetically by the name of the sender, and then chronologically, the correspondence includes several hundred letters to and from Nash. More extensive correspondence is found with the following institutions and persons: Henry Lewis Bullen, Charles W. Clark, William Andrews Clark, Jr., Templeton Crocker, William Randolph Hearst, the firm of Hübel und Denck, Edwin Markham, the Montana School of Mines, A. Edward Newton, Francis Neylan, Occidental College, Frank W. Riley, Bruce Rogers, the University of California, the University of Oregon, Dr. Otto Vollbehr, the Reverend Edward J. Whelan, and Father Henry Woods. A separate section of correspondence, labelled Miscellaneous Correspondence, includes single letters from a variety of individuals. A scrapbook entitled *Blair-Murdock*, which was apparently kept by Nash, contains correspondence and clippings relating to Nash's brief tenure with that organization.

COPY, PROOF, AND LETTERS

This collection is far from complete. Missing, for example, are the copy and proof of all of the Clark Christmas books and the two Hearst books. For some of these titles, correspondence is also included. For the last ten titles listed in this section, holdings are only partial and are so indicated.

Complete:

Joseph Addison. *Trial of the Wine Brewers*
BeneDictum Benedicte
Boccaccio. *The Life of Dante*
Elizabeth Barrett Browning. *Sonnets from the Portuguese*
Henry Lewis Bullen. *Nicolas Jenson*
Cobden-Sanderson and the Doves Press
Dante Alighieri. *The Divine Comedy*
Eugene Field. *Dibdin's Ghost*
———. *Little Willie*
Bret Harte. *Dickens in Camp*
Louis Honig. *The Arrogant Youth*
Edwin Markham. *The Man with the Hoe*
H. L. Mencken. *George Sterling Memorial*
A. Edward Newton. *Mr. Strahan's Dinner Party*
Edwin O'Day. *James Wood Coffroth*
Robert Louis Stevenson. *Silverado Squatters*
W. Irving Way. *Migratory Books*
Father Henry Woods. *Laudes Virgilianae*
William Butler Yeats. *The Lake Isle of Innisfree*

Partial Holdings:

Witter Byner. *A Canticle of Praise*. letters
———. *The New World*. letters
Ecclesiastes or the Preacher. copy and letters
Bret Harte. *The Heathen Chinee*. proof
John E. Hasty. *If It Were Today*. letters
Richard Hovey. *Barney McGee*. letters
John Henry Nash. *In Mellow Mood*. letters
To Remember Ray Coyle. letters
Leonie Belle Weeks. *Leaves in the Sun*. proof and copy
Tania C. Whitman. *Poems*. proof

Miscellaneous

Included in this section are typewritten addresses delivered by Nash (see under "Nash" in the manuscripts section of the bibliography), a collection of photographs which relate to Nash's career, three large scrapbooks containing clippings from newspapers and periodicals, three guest books in which are inscribed the names of visitors to his library when it was located in San Francisco and in Eugene, a guest book for his Berkeley home, copies of the honorary degrees he received, autographed testimonials presented to Nash, and the papal blessing.

NOTES

NOTES TO CHAPTER I

[1] *Sunday Oregonian* (Portland), May 24, 1936.
[2] *Inland Printer*, XI (May, 1893), 155.
[3] Harold D. Carew, "John Henry Nash, Printer," *Touring Topics*, XXIX (July, 1929), 32.
[4] *Maple Leaf*, XIX (Dec., 1925), 224.
[5] *Sunday Oregonian* (Portland), May 24, 1936.
[6] Letter, Mrs. K. D. Barnes, Denver Public Library, Jan. 9, 1968.

NOTES TO CHAPTER II

[1] Elbert Hubbard, *The Panama Exposition* (San Francisco: Panama-Pacific International Exposition, 1915), p. [16].
[2] Karl Baedeker, *The United States with an Excursion into Mexico* (Leipsic: K. Baedeker, 1893), p. 430.
[3] During the period 1900 to 1905 only 428 of the 46,590 American imprints listed in *Publishers' Weekly* were published in San Francisco. See Rocco Crachi, *Book Publishing in San Francisco, 1900–1905 Inclusive* (typed MS), p. 1. From January to April, 1906, only ten San Francisco imprints are listed in *Publishers' Weekly*. See Ronald Silvera, *Book Publishing in San Francisco, 1906* (typed MS), p. 2.
[4] Haywood H. Hunt, "California—the Center of Fine Printing," *California Journal of Development*, XXI (Nov., 1931), 10.
[5] Edwin Bosqui, *Memoirs* (Oakland: Holmes, 1952), p. xxii.
[6] Stylus [pseud. of William Loy], "Bosqui Engraving and Printing Company," *Inland Printer*, XVIII (Nov., 1896), 187.
[7] Stylus, *loc. cit.*
[8] Charles A. Murdock, "History of Printing in San Francisco," *Pacific Printer and Publisher*, XXXIV (Oct., 1925), 262.
[9] *Inland Printer*, XII (Feb., 1894), 392.
[10] *Crocker-Langley San Francisco Directory for Year Commencing April 1896* (San Francisco: H. S. Crocker Co., 1896), p. 1165.
[11] Joseph FauntLeRoy, *John Henry Nash Printer* (Oakland: Westgate Press, 1948), p. 3.
[12] *Crocker-Langley San Francisco Directory for Year Commencing May 1899* (San Francisco: H. S. Crocker Co., 1899), p. 1281.
[13] *Inland Printer*, XVIII (Oct., 1896), 88; "artistic composition . . . and the presswork is without fault," and XIX (June, 1897), 426–427: "Your specimens are truly artistic in composition with exquisite presswork and harmonious color arrangement. The unique and beautiful presswork on the half tones, together with the artistic composition, are most convincing proofs of the ability of the E. D. Taylor Print Shop to handle that and all other classes of printing in the most satisfactory manner."
[14] *Impressions*, II (Nov., 1901), 106.
[15] *Impressions Quarterly*, III (Sept., 1902), 70–71.
[16] *Inland Printer*, XXVII (Apr., 1901), 98.
[17] *Crocker-Langley San Francisco Directory for Year Commencing May, 1900* (San Francisco: H. S. Crocker Co., 1900), p. 1277.
[18] *Impressions*, II (Oct., 1901), 80.
[19] *Ibid.*
[20] *Inland Printer*, XXV (June, 1900), 406.

21 *Impressions Quarterly*, I (March, 1902), 22.

22 *Ibid.*, III (Sept., 1902), [76].

23 *Publishers' Trade List Annual for 1907* (New York: Publishers' Weekly, 1907), Paul Elder Section, p. [1].

24 *Interview between John Henry Nash and Emil Labhard over Radio Station KFBK, Sacramento, Calif.* (typed MS), p. 4.

25 Charles Keeler, *San Francisco and Thereabout* (San Francisco: California Promotion Committee, 1903), p. 40.

26 Paul Elder, *Random Notes on Paul Elder's Book Shop* (typed MS, *Gertrude Atherton Collection*, Bancroft Library), p. 2.

27 Keeler, *loc. cit.*

28 Gertrude Atherton, *My San Francisco* (Indianapolis: Bobbs-Merrill, 1946), p. 76.

29 George French, "With the Bookmakers," *American Printer*, XL (May, 1905), 238.

30 John Henry Nash, *Address before the San Francisco Advertising Club, May 7, 1925* (typed MS), pp. 8–10.

31 *Messrs. Paul Elder and Company Cordially Extend You an Invitation to Visit Their Arts and Crafts Book Room* ([New York: P. Elder, May, 1907]), p. [2].

32 Quoted in Charles A. Murdock, "An Appreciation of the Work of John Henry Nash, as Reflected in the Exhibition of Paul Elder and Company, San Francisco, Cal.," *American Bulletin*, I (Nov., 1910), 2.

33 Lewis C. Gandy, "Modern Commercial Typography," *Graphic Arts and Crafts Yearbook*, II (1908), 123.

34 Edmund G. Gress, "Typography of Books," *American Printer*, XLVII (Oct., 1908), 204–205.

35 Edmund G. Gress, "Catalogs," *American Printer*, XLVII (Jan., 1909), 582–583.

36 Nash, *Address*, p. 12.

37 *Ibid.*

38 *American Printer*, LV (June, 1913), 631.

39 *Publishers' Weekly*, LXXV (Jan. 2, 1909), 13.

40 Quoted in *Publishers' Weekly*, LXXVI (Aug. 14, 1909), 388.

41 Murdock, "An Appreciation," p. 2.

42 John Henry Nash, "Making Good Books," *American Bulletin*, n.s., no. 9 (Jan., 1911), 7.

43 *Taylor and Taylor Pay Roll Sheets August 5, 1911 to Dec. 26, 1914 Inclusive. (Taylor and Taylor Archives*, Edward C. Kemble Collections, California Historical Society Library).

44 Quoted in Wallace Irwin, *A Tragedy in Printer's Ink* (San Francisco: Taylor, Nash & Taylor, 1913), p. 2.

45 Letter from Henry L. Bullen to Nash, Dec. 30, 1912.

46 *Printing Art*, XIX (June, 1912), 305–312.

47 Letter from Henry L. Bullen to Nash, Jan. 12, 1914.

48 *Inland Printer*, LVI (Nov., 1915), 219.

49 See *TNT Imprint*, March, 1915, p. 11; and May, 1915, p. 4; and *Printing Art*, XXII (Nov., 1913), 199, 202; (Dec., 1913), facing 284; XXIV (Oct., 1914), 117–124; "Fitness in Newspaper Advertising" (Jan., 1915), 423–428; XXV (June, 1915), 281; XXVI (Sept., 1915), 50.

50 Haywood H. Hunt, "Recollections of San Francisco Printers," typed transcript of tape-recorded interviews conducted by Ruth Teiser, University of California Bancroft Library Regional Oral History Office, (Berkeley, 1966), p. 10.

51 Nash, *Address*, p. 15.

52 *Pacific Printer and Publisher*, XIV (July, 1915), 32.

53 U. S. Dist. Ct. (N. D. Cal.) Crim. 5744, 5750.

NOTES TO CHAPTER III

[1] A. H. McQuilkin in the *Inland Printer*, XLII (Feb., 1909), 689. An earlier statement, this one in reference to the entire state of California, gives an equally negative appraisal: "If one is a successful business man in California he can succeed in any part of the world, for it takes more hard work, economy, skill, industry and brains to transact business here than elsewhere. The competition is very severe and bitter; the chances of success small and the chances of defeat great." *Western Printer*, I (Apr., 1901), 60.

[2] John Henry Nash, *Address before the San Francisco Advertising Club, May 7, 1925* (typed MS), p. 15.

[3] See for example the *Inland Printer*, XLVIII (Oct., 1911), 83; and *Printing Art*, XVIII (Oct., 1911), 115.

[4] Nash placed the amount at $3,000 and $4,000 in two different addresses delivered in 1925. See his *Address*, p. 16, and his "Co-operation between Organized Advertising and Publicity Groups for the Development, Expansion and Prosperity of American Industries and Business," *Photo-Engravers Bulletin*, XV (Aug., 1925), 157. When faced with this discrepancy, Nell O'Day, Nash's librarian and biographer, apparently decided to split the difference. She places the amount at $3,500. See her "Dr. John Henry Nash," *Inland Printer*, CII (Dec., 1938), 32.

[5] *Inland Printer*, LVIII (Oct., 1916), 72–73.

[6] Letter from Edwin Markham to Albert Bender, Aug. 2, 1915. Quoted in the Book Club of California's announcement of *The Man with the Hoe*.

[7] Letter from T. J. Cobden-Sanderson to Nash, March 7, 1917. Quoted in the Book Club of California's announcement of *The Ideal Book*.

[8] Letter from Henry L. Bullen to Nash, Dec. 15, 1916.

[9] Letter from George Sterling to Nash, Dec. 25, 1916.

[10] David Magee, *The Hundredth Book* (San Francisco: Book Club of California, 1958), pp. 3–5.

[11] *Pacific Printer and Publisher*, XVIII (Nov., 1917), 184.

[12] *Ibid.*, XIX (Jan., 1918), 152.

[13] *Santa Barbara News*, Feb. 27, 1931.

[14] *Inland Printer*, LIX (June, 1917), 368; and LX (Feb., 1918), insert between pp. 640 and 641.

[15] *Pacific Printer and Publisher*, XVII (Apr., 1917), 142.

[16] Letter from W. Irving Way to Nash, Apr. 7, 1917.

[17] *Pacific Printer and Publisher*, XVII (Apr., 1917), 142.

[18] *San Francisco Chronicle*, Jan. 5, 1919.

[19] Letter from Henry L. Bullen to Nash, Jan. 6, 1919.

[20] *Inland Printer*, LXIV (March, 1920), 714.

[21] *Pacific Printer and Publisher*, XVIII (Nov., 1917), 184.

NOTES TO CHAPTER IV

[1] *San Francisco Examiner*, Oct. 15, 1927.

[2] *Eugene Register Guard*, July 8, 1938.

[3] *Peninsulan*, III (May, 1936), 28.

[4] Joseph FauntLeRoy, *John Henry Nash Printer* (Oakland: Westgate Press, 1948), p. 12.

[5] *Pacific Printer and Publisher*, XLIX (Apr., 1933), 39.

[6] *Ibid.*, and Lawton Kennedy, "A Life in Printing," typed transcript of a tape-recorded interview conducted by Ruth Teiser, University of California Bancroft Library Regional Oral History Office, (Berkeley, 1967), p. 50.

[7] FauntLeRoy, *op. cit.*, p. 18.

[8] Haywood H. Hunt, "More about John Henry Nash," *Inland Printer*, CIII (May, 1939), 44; and *Monthly Letter*, Limited Editions Club, No. 66 (Nov., 1934), 2.

[9] FauntLeRoy, *op. cit.*, pp. 12–13.

[10] Haywood H. Hunt, "Recollections of San Francisco Printers," typed transcript of tape-recorded interviews conducted by Ruth Teiser, University of California Bancroft Library Regional Oral History Office, (Berkeley, 1966), p. 13; and telephone conversation with Lawton Kennedy, July 11, 1968.

[11] Nell O'Day, "Dr. John Henry Nash, Part III," *Inland Printer*, CII (Feb., 1939), 38.

[12] *Monthly Letter*, Limited Editions Club, No. 66 (Nov., 1934), 2.

[13] Kennedy, *op. cit.*, p. 51.

[14] Hunt, "Recollections," *loc. cit.*

[15] *Ibid.*

[16] Hunt, "More," p. 43.

[17] Kennedy, *op. cit.*, p. 59.

[18] *Interview between John Henry Nash and Emil Labhard over Radio Station KFBK, Sacramento, Calif.* (typed MS), p. 5.

[19] FauntLeRoy, *op. cit.*, p. 25.

[20] *John Henry Nash, Printer* (Eugene, Oregon: J. H. Nash Fine Arts Press, 1940), p. [5].

[21] Letter from Henry L. Bullen to William Andrews Clark, Jr., Jan. 9, 1931.

[22] FauntLeRoy, *op. cit.*, p. 14.

[23] John Henry Nash, "Co-operation between Organized Advertising and Publicity Groups for the Development, Expansion and Prosperity of American Industries and Business," *Photo-Engravers Bulletin*, XV (Aug., 1925), 156.

[24] Letter from Arthur Scribner to Nash, Apr. 16, 1924.

[25] FauntLeRoy, *op. cit.*, pp. 47–48.

[26] The wording of the following agreement is similar to that of the others: "The money received from the sale of the book to be kept in a special account and paid over to Mr. Nash at the end of each month." *Minutes*, Book Club of California, Dec. 10, 1924 (*Archives*, Book Club of California).

[27] *The Argonaut*, XCII (March 10, 1923), 146.

[28] FauntLeRoy, *op. cit.*, p. 59.

[29] *Minutes*, Book Club of California, Sept. 13, 1929 (*Archives*, Book Club of California).

[30] FauntLeRoy, *op. cit.*, p. 52.

[31] *New York Times Book Review*, June 13, 1926.

[32] *Inland Printer*, LXXXIII (Aug., 1929), 68.

[33] Letter from Nash to Caspar W. Hodgson, Nov. 13, 1923.

[34] Letter from Hodgson to Nash, Nov. 26, 1923.

[35] Letter from George W. Jones to Nash, Oct. 1, 1929.

[36] FauntLeRoy, *op. cit.*, p. 38.

[37] *Prospectus* for Dante's *Divine Comedy* ([San Francisco: J. H. Nash, 1928]), pp. [1]–[2].

[38] *Sunday Oregonian* (Portland), May 24, 1936.

[39] Letter from Morgan Shepard to Nash, Sept. 24, 1929.

[40] Letter from Mitchell Kennerly to Nash, Apr. 4, 1929.

[41] Letter from Henry L. Bullen to Nash, Sept. 24, 1929.

[42] Letter from A. Edward Newton to Flodden Heron, Oct. 5, 1930 (*Newton–Heron Correspondence*, Bancroft Library).

[43] Letter from Nell O'Day to Henry L. Bullen, Feb. 5, 1930: "Mr. Nash feels that the Goudy, Rollins crowd is actively hostile to him. Some years ago he made a speech in New York and Goudy signified his disapproval of it by making a sort of clucking."

44 *Saturday Review of Literature,* VI (Dec. 7, 1929), 549.

45 *Ibid.,* (Feb. 8, 1930), 724.

46 *Ibid.,* pp. 724–725.

47 *Ibid.*

48 Kennedy, *op. cit.,* p. 165.

49 Nash, "Co-operation," p. 158.

50 John Henry Nash, *Printing, An Address Delivered at a Luncheon of the Advertising Club of Los Angeles, January 15, 1924* (typed MS).

51 *The Informant,* VI (Apr., 1924), 13.

52 Edgar Allan Poe, *Tamerlane* (San Francisco: J. H. Nash, 1923), p. [iii].

53 For example, he turned over the million dollars he made on the stock market during World War I to the Belgian government. See "William Andrews Clark," *National Cyclopaedia of American Biography,* XXV (1936), 301.

54 *Report of the First Decade, 1934–1944,* William Andrews Clark Memorial Library (Los Angeles: University of California Press, 1946), p. 14.

55 Letter from George M. Millard to Nash, Sept. 9, 1916.

56 Letter from Robert E. Cowan to Nash, Aug. 4, 1917.

57 FauntLeRoy, *op. cit.,* p. 16.

58 Percy Bysshe Shelley, *Adonais* (San Francisco: J. H. Nash, 1922), p. [iii].

59 Receipt. All subsequent figures of Nash's bills to Clark are from receipts in the *Nash Archives* unless otherwise indicated and are not footnoted.

60 *John Henry Nash, Address before the San Francisco Advertising Club, May 7, 1925* (typed MS), p. 21.

61 James V. Murray, "John Henry Nash Plans Palace of Printing Art to Be Built When He Reaches Age of 60," *Ben Franklin and Western Printing,* XXVII (May 15, 1926), 27.

62 Letter from Nash to William Andrews Clark, Jr., Oct. 28, 1926.

63 Letter from Henry L. Bullen to William Andrews Clark, Jr., quoted in Edward F. O'Day, *John Henry Nash, the Aldus of San Francisco* (San Francisco: San Francisco Bay Cities Club of Printing House Craftsmen, 1928), pp. [11]–[12].

64 Letter from Henry L. Bullen to William Andrews Clark, Jr., Jan. 9, 1931.

65 *Ibid.*

66 *John Henry Nash to William Andrews Clark, Jr., Friend* ([San Francisco: J. H. Nash, n.d.]). Clark volunteered to subscribe for ten sets and pay Nash the full amount of two thousand dollars.

67 A. Edward Newton, "The Course of Empire," *Atlantic Monthly,* CL (Sept., 1932), 301.

68 Nell O'Day, "Dr. John Henry Nash, Part II," *Inland Printer,* CII (Jan., 1939), 23–24.

69 Agreement between Nash and William Randolph Hearst, Apr. 15, 1927.

70 Nell O'Day, *op. cit.,* p. 25.

71 *San Francisco Examiner,* March 8, 1929. Lawton Kennedy has told the author that he believes the printing was done in San Francisco, not in Germany.

72 W. A. Swanberg, *Citizen Hearst, a Biography* (New York: Scribner's Sons, 1961), p. 322.

73 *San Francisco Examiner,* March 7, 1929.

74 *Announcing a Public Showing ... Art Gallery Mills College, March Fourteen Nineteen Hundred & Twenty-Nine* ([San Francisco: J. H. Nash, 1929]), p. [2].

75 Ads placed in Elder and Shepard's magazine show that the shop carried such rare items as a Shakespeare First Folio, a *Nuremberg Chronicle,* and examples of fine printers from John Baskerville to Charles Ricketts, and the publications of Thomas B. Mosher. See *Personal Impressions,* II (March, 1900), [16], and (May, 1900), 49; and *Impressions,* I (Oct., 1900), 140, and (Apr., 1901), 246.

76 *TNT Imprint,* March, 1915, p. 1.

[77] *Inland Printer*, LX (March, 1918), 759.

[78] John Henry Nash, "Higher Standards in the Printing Business," *Pacific Printer and Publisher*, XXI (June, 1919), 245.

[79] Frederic W. Goudy, "What Printing Is," *Ars Typographica*, I (Summer, 1918), 38.

[80] Nash, *Address*, p. 23.

[81] Release from a newspaper conference, Eugene, Oregon, 1925, in Nash Scrapbook.

[82] *San Francisco Examiner* and *San Francisco Chronicle*, both June 26, 1927.

[83] *San Matean*, Apr. 9, 1931.

[84] *Sierra Madre News*, Jan. 6, 1928.

[85] *San Matean*, Apr. 9, 1931.

[86] A. W. Pollard, "How to Stimulate Good Printing," *Printing Art*, XIV (Nov., 1909), 170.

[87] Letter from Joseph FauntLeRoy to Nash, Feb. 13, 1921.

[88] A. Edward Newton, *The Greatest Book in the World, and Other Papers* (Boston: Little, Brown, 1925), p. 45.

[89] FauntLeRoy, *op. cit.*, p. 26.

[90] *The Needle*, II (Dec., 1922), 6.

[91] Letter from George W. Jones to Nash, Dec. 1, 1922.

[92] Letter from Stanley Morison to Nash, July 25, 1924.

[93] Letters to Nash from W. Irving Way, March 12, 1924; from Jerome Kern, July 25, 1924; and from Henry L. Bullen, Nov. 9, 1922.

[94] Letter from Bruce Rogers to Nash, Dec. 9, 1922.

[95] Letter from Bruce Rogers to Nash, Feb. 11, 1925.

[96] FauntLeRoy, *op. cit.*, p. 45.

[97] *Ibid.*

[98] *Jewish Journal*, III (Feb. 5, 1930), 2.

[99] *San Francisco Examiner*, Dec. 19, 1927.

[100] *Ad Age*, XIV (Jan. 16, 1928), [1].

NOTES TO CHAPTER V

[1] Letter from Nash to Henry L. Bullen, June 10, 1930.

[2] Letter from Flodden Heron to A. Edward Newton, Dec. 19, 1930 (*Newton–Heron Correspondence*).

[3] Joseph FauntLeRoy, *John Henry Nash Printer* (Oakland: Westgate Press, 1948), p. 44.

[4] Contract between Nash and the Book Club for the printing of A. Edward Newton, *Mr. Strahan's Dinner Party* (Archives, Book Club of California).

[5] Letter from William Andrews Clark, Jr. to Nash, Feb. 10, 1931.

[6] Letter from William Andrews Clark, Jr. to Nash, Aug. 18, 1931.

[7] *Monthly Letter*, Limited Editions Club, No. 9 (Feb., 1930), 2.

[8] Nell O'Day, *A Catalogue of Books Printed by John Henry Nash* (San Francisco: J. H. Nash, 1937), p. 78.

[9] *Fifty Books of the Year* (New York: American Institute of Graphic Arts, 1932), p. 35.

[10] Letter from Nash to Henry L. Bullen, Apr. 11, 1930.

[11] "John Henry Is Dead," *Pacific Printer and Publisher*, LXXVII (June, 1947), 22.

[12] Letter from Flodden Heron to A. Edward Newton, Apr. 1, 1931 (*Newton–Heron Correspondence*, Bancroft Library).

[13] Letter from John B. Kennedy to Nash, March 13, 1931.

[14] *Pacific Printer and Publisher*, XLV (March, 1931), 59.

[15] *Oakland Enquirer*, Feb. 12, 1921. This story announces that Nash planned to

start work on the Bible in two years and that the Book Club of California was anxious to be associated with the project.

16 Letter from Nash to Henry L. Bullen, Apr. 11, 1930.

17 FauntLeRoy, *op. cit.*, pp. 54–56.

18 Letter from Bruce Rogers to Nash, May 4, 1930.

19 Letter from Nash to Henry L. Bullen, Dec. 30, 1930.

20 *Prospectus* for the Bible ([San Francisco: J. H. Nash, 1932]), p. iv.

21 *Ibid.*, p. iv.

22 Letter from Henry L. Bullen to Nash, June 17, 1932.

23 Letter from Nash to Henry L. Bullen, June 6, 1932.

24 *Oakland Enquirer*, March 11, 1932.

25 *Pacific Printer and Publisher*, XLVIII (July, 1932), 25.

26 Letter from Nash to Mrs. Estelle Doheny, July 27, 1931.

27 *I, John Henry Nash, Printer of San Francisco, Hereby Certify and Attest That This Is the Veritable and First Set of Printer's Rough Stone Proofs . . .* ([San Francisco: J. H. Nash, 1931]).

28 FauntLeRoy, *op. cit.*, p. 57.

29 *Archives*, Book Club of California.

30 Response written on an order form from the Book Club (*Archives*, Book Club of California).

31 Letter from Nash to William Andrews Clark, Jr., March 30, 1932.

32 Letter from William Andrews Clark, Jr., to Nash, March 30, 1932.

33 Letter from Nash to William Andrews Clark, Jr., Apr. 6, 1932.

34 *San Francisco Call Bulletin*, Dec. 3, 1932.

35 *Saturday Night*, XIII (Nov. 26, 1932), 11.

36 *Pacific Printer and Publisher*, XLIX (Apr., 1933), pp. 39–40.

37 Charles McIntyre, "The Making of a Great Book," *Pacific Printer and Publisher*, LIII (March, 1935), 23.

38 Contract between Nash and Robert E. Cowan, Jan. 20, 1933.

39 *New York Times Book Review*, Sept. 2, 1934.

40 *San Francisco Chronicle*, Sept. 3, 1933.

41 *San Francisco Call Bulletin*, March 7, 1934.

42 *William Caxton*, Zellerbach Paper Company Keepsake ([San Francisco: J. H. Nash, 1934]), colophon.

43 Letter from William Andrews Clark, Jr. to Nash, May 16, 1934.

44 Contract between Nash and the Book Club, July 23, 1934 (*Archives*, Book Club of California).

45 *Fifty Books of the Year* (New York: American Institute of Graphic Arts, 1935), item 3.

46 *Ibid.*, item 31.

47 Robert Grabhorn, "Fine Printing and the Grabhorn Press," typed transcript of tape-recorded interview conducted by Ruth Teiser, University of California Bancroft Library Regional Oral History Office (Berkeley, 1968), p. 24.

48 *Fifty Books of the Year* (New York: American Institute of Graphic Arts, 1936), p. 3.

49 *San Francisco Call Bulletin*, Oct. 2, 1935.

50 *San Francisco Chronicle*, July 21, 1935.

51 Letter to the author from Mrs. Weldon C. Nichols, Feb. 21, 1968.

52 *San Francisco Call Bulletin*, Apr. 21, 1936.

53 *Inland Printer*, XCVII (May, 1936), 79.

54 *Ibid.*; and *Pacific Printer and Publisher*, LV (Apr., 1936), 40.

55 *Lincoln Heights Review*, Oct. 5, 1936.

56 *Announcement* of resumption of work ([San Francisco: J. H. Nash, 1936]).

57 *Pacific Printer and Publisher*, LVI (Oct., 1936), 42.

[58] *The Green and Gold for the Year 1937* (San Francisco: J. H. Nash, 1937), p. [85].

[59] *San Francisco Call Bulletin,* March 27, 1937.

[60] Announcement for the series ([San Francisco: J. H. Nash, 1937]).

[61] Announcement for Guillermo Prieto, *San Francisco in the Seventies* ([San Francisco: J. H. Nash, 1938]).

NOTES TO CHAPTER VI

[1] *San Franciscan,* IV (Oct., 1930), 15.

[2] *Berkeley Gazette,* May 22, 1936.

[3] *Inland Printer,* XCVII (June, 1936), 83.

[4] Nelson A. Crawford, "American University Presses," *American Mercury,* XVIII (Oct., 1929), pp. 212–213.

[5] *Morning Oregonian* (Portland), March 18, 1925.

[6] Joe D. Thomison, *A Call to Oregon's Newspaper Fraternity, March 11, 1926* ([Hood River: Committee of Nash Press Fund of the Oregon Newspaper Conference, 1926]).

[7] *Morning Register* (Eugene), March 12, 1926.

[8] *Eugene Guard,* Dec. 25, 1926.

[9] Thomison, *loc. cit.*

[10] Martin Schmitt, "John Henry Nash at the University of Oregon," *PNLA Quarterly,* XIII (July, 1949), 130.

[11] *Ibid.*

[12] See, for example, *Eugene Guard,* July 28, 1927.

[13] *Pacific Printer and Publisher,* XXXVIII (Aug., 1927), 39.

[14] *Eugene Register,* Sept. 7, 1929.

[15] *Saturday Review of Literature,* IX (June 10, 1933), 647.

[16] *Inland Printer,* XCI (July, 1933), 37.

[17] *Pacific Printer and Publisher,* C (Nov., 1937), 72.

[18] *Eugene Register Guard,* March 22, 1938.

[19] *San Francisco News,* March 22, 1938.

[20] Report to the Librarian of the University of Oregon (typed MS). Oregon, 43; Washington State, 38; University of Southern California, 36; Stanford University, 35; University of California, 23; University of Texas, 9.

[21] Schmitt, *op. cit.,* p. 131.

[22] *San Francisco Chronicle,* May 10, 1938.

[23] *Oregon Daily Emerald* (Eugene), Aug. 16, 1938.

[24] Christmas broadside ([Eugene: J. H. Nash, 1938]).

[25] *Arizona Republic* (Phoenix), March 28, 1939.

[26] Schmitt, *loc. cit.*

[27] *Inland Printer,* CVII (July, 1941), 42.

[28] *Ibid.,* CII (March, 1939), 38.

[29] *Oregon Daily Journal* (Portland), Feb. 9, 1939.

[30] Robert Grabhorn, "Fine Printing and the Grabhorn Press," typed transcript of a tape-recorded interview conducted by Ruth Teiser, University of California Bancroft Library Regional Oral History Office, (Berkeley, 1968), p. 73.

NOTES TO CHAPTER VII

[1] Letter to the author from Mrs. Weldon C. Nichols, Feb. 21, 1968.

[2] Telephone conversation with Lawton Kennedy, July 11, 1968.

[3] *Pacific Printer and Publisher,* LXXI (June, 1944), 32; and *Quarterly Newsletter,* Book Club of California, XXI (Winter, 1955), 16.

4 *San Francisco Chronicle* and *San Francisco Examiner*, May 25, 1947; *Oakland Tribune*, May 25, 1947; *Berkeley Daily Gazette*, May 26, 1947; *New York Times*, May 25, 1947; *Inland Printer*, CXIX (July, 1947), 31–32; *Pacific Printer and Publisher*, LXXVII (June, 1947), 21–22.

NOTES TO CHAPTER VIII

1 Letter from Henry L. Bullen printed in *Saturday Review of Literature*, VI (Feb. 8, 1929), 724.

2 Jane Grabhorn, "The Colt Press," typed transcript of a tape-recorded interview conducted by Ruth Teiser, University of California Bancroft Library Regional Oral History Office, (Berkeley, 1966), p. 16.

3 Robert Grabhorn, "Fine Printing and the Grabhorn Press," typed transcript of a tape-recorded interview conducted by Ruth Teiser, University of California Bancroft Library Regional Oral History Office, (Berkeley, 1968), p. 23.

4 Adrian Wilson, "Printing and Book Designing," typed transcript of a tape-recorded interview conducted by Ruth Teiser, University of California Bancroft Library Regional Oral History Office, (Berkeley, 1966), p. 94.

5 *Quarto-millenary; The First 250 Publications and the First 25 Years, 1929–1954, of the Limited Editions Club* (New York: Limited Editions Club, 1959), p. 10.

6 *Monthly Letter*, Limited Editions Club, No. [?] (Nov., 1931), 1.

7 *Monthly Letter*, Limited Editions Club, No. 66 (Nov., 1934), 1.

8 *Monthly Letter*, Limited Editions Club, No. 91 (Dec., 1936), [1].

9 Stanley Morison, *Modern Fine Printing* (London: Benn, 1925), p. xi.

10 Oliver Simon, Beatrice Warde, and Julius Rodenberg, *Printing of To-day, an Illustrated Survey of Post-War Typography in Europe and the United States* (London: P. Davies, 1928), p. 53.

11 *Ibid.*, p. 51.

12 *Quarto-millenary*, p. 10.

13 *Saturday Review of Literature*, IX (Jan. 7, 1933), 370.

14 Edwin Grabhorn, "Recollections of the Grabhorn Press," typed transcript of a tape-recorded interview conducted by Ruth Teiser, University of California Bancroft Library Regional Oral History Office, (Berkeley, 1968), p. 74.

15 John Henry Nash, "In Defense of Fnely Printed Books," *American Printer*, LXXXIV (June, 1927), 52–53.

16 Letter from Nash to Caspar W. Hodgson, undated.

17 Hellmut Lehmann-Haupt, *The Book in America* (New York: Bowker, 1952), pp. 285–286.

18 Sir Francis Meynell, *English Printed Books* (London: Collins, 1946), p. 33.

19 Albert Sperisen, "San Francisco Area Printers, 1925–1965," typed transcript of tape-recorded interviews conducted by Ruth Teiser, University of California Bancroft Library Regional Oral History Office, (Berkeley, 1966), p. 66.

20 *Oakland Enquirer*, Aug. 27, 1921.

21 Harold D. Carew, "John Henry Nash, Printer," *Touring Topics*, XXIX (July, 1929), 48.

22 *Ibid.*

23 *Salem Statesman*, May 31, 1930.

24 *San Francisco Grocer*, Feb. 10, 1922.

25 *Oakland Enquirer*, Jan. 17, 1920.

26 *An Appraisal of the William Morris Case in the Graphic Arts Library of Los Angeles* (N.p.: n.p., n.d.). See Nash Scrapbook.

27 Frona E. W. Colburn, "John Henry Nash, Master Printer," *Overland Monthly*, n.s., LXXXVII (June, 1929), 179.

28 Lawton Kennedy, "A Life in Printing," typed transcript of a tape-recorded

interview conducted by Ruth Teiser, University of California Bancroft Library Regional Oral History Office, (Berkeley, 1967), p. 63.

[29] Elbert Hubbard, *Good Men and Great,* Little Journeys to the Homes of the Great, I (New York: W. H. Wise & Co., 1916), p. xxvi.

[30] Edwin Wolf and John F. Fleming, *Rosenbach, a Biography* (Cleveland: World Publishing Co., 1960), p. 236.

[31] Haywood H. Hunt, "Recollections of San Francisco Printers," typed transcript of tape-recorded interviews conducted by Ruth Teiser, University of California Bancroft Library Regional Oral History Office, (Berkeley, 1966), p. 23.

[32] Robert Grabhorn, *op. cit.,* p. 23.

[33] Letter from James Johnson to Nash, Oct. 23, 1925.

[34] *The Needle,* II (Dec., 1922), 6.

[35] Haywood H. Hunt, "John Henry Nash, Master Craftsman," *The Pi-Box,* May, 1936, p. [1].

[36] Letter from Ward Ritchie to Nash, May 9, 1940.

[37] *Sierra Madre News,* Jan. 6, 1928.

[38] *A Book of Designations: A Message to Men and Women of Vision* (typed MS with architectural plans).

[39] "John Henry Nash Tours Europe," *Pacific Printer and Publisher,* XL (July, 1928), 38.

[40] *San Francisco Call Bulletin,* March 14, 1933.

SELECTED BIBLIOGRAPHY

The Selected Bibliography includes manuscripts and publications cited in the corpus of this study and works which were used but not cited which have a direct bearing upon the topic.

MANUSCRIPTS

COLLECTED

Book Club of California Archives. Book Club of California, San Francisco.

John Henry Nash Archives. Rare Books and Special Collections Room, University of California Library, Berkeley.

Newton–Heron Correspondence. Bancroft Library, University of California, Berkeley.

Taylor and Taylor Archives. Edward C. Kemble Collections, California Historical Society Library, San Francisco.

INDIVIDUAL ITEMS

CRACHI, ROCCO. *Book Publishing in San Francisco, 1900–1905 Inclusive.* Typed MS, in the possession of Prof. Fredric J. Mosher, School of Librarianship, University of California, Berkeley.

ELDER, PAUL. *Random Notes on Paul Elder's Book Shop.* Typed MS, Gertrude Atherton Collection, Bancroft Library, University of California, Berkeley.

FARQUHAR, FRANCIS P. "Comments on Some Bay Area Fine Printers." Typed transcript of a tape-recorded interview conducted by Ruth Teiser, University of California Bancroft Library Regional Oral History Office, Berkeley, 1968.

——. "On Accountancy, Mountaineering, and the National Parks." Typed transcript of tape-recorded interviews conducted by Willa K. Baum, University of California General Library Regional Cultural History Project, Berkeley, 1958. In Bancroft Library.

GRABHORN, EDWIN. "Recollections of the Grabhorn Press." Typed transcript of a tape-recorded interview conducted by Ruth Teiser, University of California Bancroft Library Regional Oral History Office, Berkeley, 1968.

GRABHORN, JANE. "The Colt Press." Typed transcript of a tape-recorded interview conducted by Ruth Teiser, University of California Bancroft Library Regional Oral History Office, Berkeley, 1966.

GRABHORN, ROBERT. "Fine Printing and the Grabhorn Press." Typed transcript of a tape-recorded interview conducted by Ruth Teiser, University of California Bancroft Library Regional Oral History Office, Berkeley, 1968.

HARDING, GEORGE. *Charles A. Murdock, Printer and Citizen: An Appraisal.* Typed MS, in the possession of Mr. Roger Levenson of the Tamalpais Press, Berkeley. The work is scheduled to be published by Mr. Levenson.

HUNT, HAYWOOD H. "Recollections of San Francisco Printers." Typed transcript of tape-recorded interviews conducted by Willa K. Baum, University of California General Library Regional Cultural History Project, Berkeley, 1958. In Bancroft Library.

KENNEDY, LAWTON. "A Life in Printing." Typed transcript of a tape-recorded interview conducted by Ruth Teiser, University of California Bancroft Library Regional Oral History Office, Berkeley, 1967.

LEWIS, OSCAR. "Literary San Francisco." Typed transcript of tape-recorded interviews conducted by Ruth Teiser and Catherine Harrun, University of California Bancroft Library Regional Oral History Office, Berkeley, 1965.

NASH, JOHN HENRY. *Address before the San Francisco Advertising Club, May 7, 1925.* Typed MS, *John Henry Nash Archives*, Rare Books and Special Collections Room, University of California Library, Berkeley.

———. *Interview between John Henry Nash and Emil Labhard over Radio Station KFBK, Sacramento, Calif.* Typed MS, *John Henry Nash Archives*, Rare Books and Special Collections Room, University of California Library, Berkeley.

———. *Printing, An Address Delivered at a Luncheon of the Advertising Club of Los Angeles, January 15, 1924.* Typed MS, *John Henry Nash Archives*, Rare Books and Special Collections Room, University of California Library, Berkeley.

SILVERA, RONALD. *Book Publishing in San Francisco, 1906.* Typed MS, in the possession of Prof. Fredric J. Mosher, School of Librarianship, University of California, Berkeley.

SPERISEN, ALBERT. "San Francisco Area Printers, 1925–1965." Typed transcript of tape-recorded interviews conducted by Ruth Teiser, University of California Bancroft Library Regional Oral History Office, Berkeley, 1966.

WILSON, ADRIAN. "Printing and Book Designing." Typed transcript of a tape-recorded interview conducted by Ruth Teiser, University of California Bancroft Library Regional Oral History Office, Berkeley, 1966.

PUBLICATIONS

ARTICLES AND BOOKS

ACKERMAN, PHYLLIS. "Where Printing Is An Art; John Henry Nash in His Little Shop in San Francisco Revives the Old Standards of Typography," *International Studio*, LXXVIII (Oct., 1923), 32–36.

ALLEN, MARION B. "The Tomoyé Press," Book Club of California *Quarterly News-Letter*, XVI (Fall, 1951), 84–88.

ATHERTON, GERTRUDE. *My San Francisco.* Indianapolis: Bobbs-Merrill, 1946.

BAEDEKER, KARL. *The United States with an Excursion into Mexico.* Leipsic: K. Baedeker, 1893.

BEER, THOMAS. *The Mauve Decade.* New York: A. A. Knopf, 1926.

BOSQUI, EDWIN. *Memoirs.* Oakland: Holmes, 1952.

BULLEN, HENRY L. "Is Printing an Art?" *American Bulletin,* 2d series, No. 14 (Dec., 1915), 4.

———. "Printers: Mechanical and Intellectual," *American Bulletin,* 2d series, No. 18 (June, 1918), 6–10.

BURGESS, GELETT. *Bayside Bohemia: Fin de Siècle San Francisco & Its Little Magazines.* San Francisco: Book Club of California, 1954.

CAREW, HAROLD D. "John Henry Nash, Printer," *Touring Topics,* XXIX (July, 1929), 32–34, 48.

CARPENTER, KENNETH J. "BR to JHN," Book Club of California *Quarterly News-Letter,* XXIII (Spring, 1958), 29–39.

CLARK, WILLIAM ANDREWS, JR. "An Introduction," *in* Edgar Allan Poe, *Tamerlane.* San Francisco: J. H. Nash, 1923. Pp. ii–xli.

———. "Introduction," *in* Percy Bysshe Shelley, *Adonais.* San Francisco: J. H. Nash, 1922. Pp. [v]–x.

———. "A Note," *in* Oliver Goldsmith, *The Deserted Village.* San Francisco: J. H. Nash, 1926. Pp. [v]–xii.

COLBURN, FRONA E. W. "John Henry Nash, Master Printer," *Overland Monthly,* n.s., LXXXVII (June, 1929), 179.

CRAWFORD, NELSON A. "American University Presses," *American Mercury,* XVIII (Oct., 1929), 210–214.

Crocker-Langley San Francisco Directory for Year Commencing April 1896. San Francisco: H. S. Crocker Co., 1896.

Crocker-Langley San Francisco Directory for Year Commencing May 1899. San Francisco: H. S. Crocker Co., 1899.

Crocker-Langley San Francisco Directory for Year Commencing May, 1900. San Francisco: H. S. Crocker Co., 1900.

Crocker-Langley San Francisco Directory for the Year Commencing May, 1904. San Francisco: H. S. Crocker Co., 1904.

DANIELS, MARK. "A Home Built for a Pair of Doors. The Home of John Henry Nash, M.A., Litt. D., Hon. AIA," *California Arts and Architecture,* XLVI (Oct., 1934), 18–19.

EVANS, CHARLES W. "John Henry Nash: The Last Ten Years," *California Librarian,* XXIII (July, 1962), 139–143, 159.

FAUNTLEROY, JOSEPH. *John Henry Nash Printer.* Oakland: Westgate Press, 1948.

FIELD, OLIVER T. "The John Henry Nash Library," *PNLA Quarterly,* IV (Apr., 1940), 99–101.

FRENCH, GEORGE. "With the Bookmakers," *American Printer,* XL (May, 1905), 238–239.

GALLATIN, A. E. "Modern Fine Printing in America," *American Magazine of Art,* XI (Nov. 1920), 461–466.

GANDY, LEWIS C. "Modern Commercial Typography," *Graphic Arts and Crafts* Yearbook, II (1918), 117–[134].

GOUDY, FREDERIC W. "What Printing Is," *Ars Typographica*, I (Summer, 1918), 37–40.

GRALBO, V. J. "A Printer in Cap and Gown," *Inland Printer*, LXXIX (July, 1927), 617–618.

GRESS, EDMUND G. "Catalogs," *American Printer*, XLVII (Jan., 1909), 582–583.

———. "Nash and the Oregon Newspapers," *American Printer*, XCIV (May, 1927), 82.

———. "The Typographer and His Advantages," *American Printer*, L (May 1910), 337–341.

———. "Typography of Books," *American Printer*, XLVII (Oct., 1908), 204–205.

HART, JAMES D. *Fine Printing in California*. California Library Association Keepsake Series, no. 1. Berkeley: California Library Association, 1960.

HASTY, JOHN E. "A Sketch of John Henry Nash, Printer," *Sunset Magazine*, LXIII (Dec., 1929), 26–27, 57.

HEDLEY, GEORGE. *Aurelia Henry Reinhardt: Portrait of a Whole Woman*. [Oakland]: Mills College, 1961.

HOLME, CHARLES, ed. *The Art of the Book, a Review of Some Recent European and American Work in Typography, Page Decoration, and Binding*. New York: The Studio Ltd., 1914.

HOWELL, JOHN. *The Friendship of Books*. San Francisco: [Grabhorn Press], 1954.

HUBBARD, ELBERT. *The Panama Exposition*. San Francisco: Panama-Pacific International Exposition, 1915.

HUNT, HAYWOOD H. "California—The Center of Fine Printing," *California Journal of Development*, XXI (Nov., 1931), 10, 40–41.

———. "John Henry Nash, Master Craftsman," *The Pi-Box*, May, 1936, pp. [1]–[2].

———. "More about John Henry Nash," *Inland Printer*, CIII (May, 1939), 43–45.

IRWIN, WALLACE. *A Tragedy in Printer's Ink*. San Francisco: Taylor, Nash and Taylor, 1913.

"John Henry Is Dead," *Pacific Printer and Publisher*, LXXVII (June, 1947), 21–22.

"John Henry Nash, Printer Extraordinary, Scholar, Artist," *Inland Printer*, CXIX (July, 1947), 31–32.

"John Henry Nash Tours Europe," *Pacific Printer and Publisher*, XL (July, 1928), 37–38.

JOYNER, GEORGE. *Fine Printing: Its Inception, Development and Practice, 1870–1895*. London: Cooper & Budd, 1895.

KEELER, CHARLES. *San Francisco and Thereabout*. San Francisco: California Promotion Committee, 1903.

KIBBEE, WALLACE. "William Doxey and 'Les Jeunes,'" Book Club of California *Quarterly News-Letter*, VI (Dec., 1938), 5–8.

Langley's San Francisco Directory for 1895. San Francisco: J. B. Painter Co., 1895.

LEHMANN-HAUPT, HELLMUT. *The Book in America.* New York: R. R. Bowker, 1952.

LEWIS, OSCAR. *Bay Window Bohemia.* New York: Doubleday, 1956.

——. *Fabulous San Simeon.* San Francisco: California Historical Society, 1958.

——. *Fine Printing in the Far West.* Orinda, Cal.: Platen Press, 1946.

——. "John Henry Nash, 1871–1947," Book Club of California *Quarterly News-Letter*, XII (Autumn, 1947), supplement.

——. *This Was San Francisco.* New York: D. McKay, 1962.

McFARLAND, J. HORACE. "What Is Fine Printing?" *Printing Art*, XL (Nov., 1922), 257–258.

McINTYRE, CHARLES. "The Making of a Great Book," *Pacific Printer and Publisher*, LIII (March, 1935), 21–23.

McQUILKIN, A. H. "Charles A. Murdock," *Inland Printer*, XLII (March, 1909), 873–875.

MAGEE, DAVID. *The Hundredth Book.* San Francisco: Book Club of California, 1958.

MANGAM, WILLIAM D. *The Clarks: An American Phenomenon.* New York: Silver Bow Press, 1941.

Messrs. Paul Elder and Company Cordially Extend You an Invitation to Visit Their Arts and Crafts Book Room. [New York: P. Elder, May, 1907].

MEYNELL, SIR FRANCIS. *English Printed Books.* London: Collins, 1946.

MIGHELS, MRS. ELLA STERLING (CLARK). *The Story of the Files; A Review of California Writers and Literature.* San Francisco: World's Fair Commission of California, 1893.

MORISON, STANLEY. *Modern Fine Printing.* London: Benn, 1925.

MURDOCK, CHARLES A. "An Appreciation of the Work of John Henry Nash, as Reflected in the Exhibition of Paul Elder and Company, San Francisco, Cal.," *American Bulletin*, I (Nov., 1910), 1–2.

——. *A Backward Glance at Eighty.* San Francisco: Elder, 1921.

——. "History of Printing in San Francisco," *Pacific Printer and Publisher*, XXXII (Aug., 1924), 118–119; (Sept., 1924), 187–188; (Oct., 1924), 258–259, 272; (Nov., 1924), 330–331; (Dec., 1924), 401, 403; XXXIII (Jan., 1925), 41–42; (Feb., 1925), 123–124; (March, 1925), 198–199; (Apr., 1925), 278–279; (May, 1925), 365–366; (June, 1925), 442–443; XXXIV (July, 1925), 35–36; (Aug., 1925), 114–115; (Sept., 1925), 186–187; (Oct., 1925), 261–262; (Nov., 1925), 340–341; (Dec., 1925), 420–421.

MURRAY, JAMES V. "John Henry Nash Plans Palace of Printing Art to Be Built When He Reaches Age of 60," *Ben Franklin and Western Printing*, XXVII (May 15, 1926), 27–28.

NASH, JOHN HENRY. "Co-operation between Organized Advertising and Publicity Groups for the Development, Expansion and Prosperity of American

Industries and Business," *Photo-Engravers Bulletin*, XV (Aug., 1925), 151–158.

——. "Higher Standards in the Printing Business," *Pacific Printer and Publisher*, XXI (June, 1919), 245–247.

——. "In Defense of Finely Printed Books," *American Printer*, LXXXIV (June, 1927), 52–53.

——. "Making Good Books," *American Bulletin*, n.s., no. 9 (Jan., 1911), 7.

——. "Materialism in Printing," *The Informant*, II (Oct., 1919), [1]–[5].

——. "What, in My Opinion, Has Been the Greatest Influence in the Progress of the Printing Industry in the Last Quarter Century?" *Inland Printer*, LXXIX (Aug., 1927), 805.

NEVILLE, AMELIA R. *The Fantastic City*. Boston: Houghton Mifflin, 1932.

NEWTON, A. EDWARD. "The Course of Empire," *Atlantic Monthly*, CL (Sept., 1932), 293–304.

——. *The Greatest Book in the World, and Other Papers*. Boston: Little, Brown, 1925.

O'BRIEN, ROBERT. "The Doxey Story," Book Club of California *Quarterly News-Letter*, XV (Spring, 1950), 27–31.

O'DAY, EDWARD F. *John Henry Nash, the Aldus of San Francisco*. San Francisco: San Francisco Bay Cities Club of Printing House Craftsmen, 1928.

——. "Theodore DeVinne's Advice to John Henry Nash, D. Litt.," *The Informant*, XII (Aug., 1930), [14]–[16].

O'DAY, NELL. *A Catalogue of Books Printed by John Henry Nash*. San Francisco: J. H. Nash, 1937.

——. "Dr. John Henry Nash," *Inland Printer*, CII (Dec., 1938), 30–34.

——. "Dr. John Henry Nash, Part II," *Inland Printer*, CII (Jan., 1939), 23–26.

——. "Dr. John Henry Nash, Part III," *Inland Printer*, CII (Feb., 1939), 35–38.

——. "Dr. John Henry Nash, Part IV," *Inland Printer*, CII (March, 1939), 35–38.

——. "San Francisco Has Its Gutenbergs," *Women's City Club Magazine*, XI (Sept., 1937), 12–13, 28.

——. "Typographic Library Honors Greatest Printer," *Pacific Printer and Publisher*, XLVI (Sept., 1931), 26–27.

O'HARA, LOUISE M. "John Henry Nash," *Publishers' Weekly*, CXIX (May 2, 1931), 2217–2220.

OLDER, MRS. FREMONT. *William Randolph Hearst, American*. New York: D. Appleton-Century, 1936.

PIELKOVA, RUTH. "Fine Printing in the West," *American Magazine of Art*, XIX (Oct., 1928), 560–562.

POLLARD, ALFRED W. "How to Stimulate Good Printing," *Printing Art*, XIV (Nov., 1909), 165–170.

PRINGLE, H. F. "Printer Who Spent Six Years on One Job," *American Magazine*, CXIV (Dec., 1932), 65.

Quarto-millenary; The First 250 Publications and First 25 Years, 1929–1954, of the Limited Editions Club. New York: Limited Editions Club, 1959.

RANSOM, WILL. *Private Presses and Their Books.* New York: R. R. Bowker, 1929.

ROSS, ISHBEL. *Ladies of the Press; The Story of Women in Journalism by an Insider.* New York: Harper, 1936.

San Francisco. Panama-Pacific International Exhibition, 1915. *Official Catalogue of Exhibitors.* San Francisco: Wahlgren, 1915. Vol. III: *Liberal Arts.*

SCHMITT, MARTIN. "John Henry Nash at the University of Oregon," *PNLA Quarterly*, XIII (July, 1949), 129–132.

SHINN, CHARLES H. "Early Books, Magazines, and Book-Making," *Overland Monthly*, 2d series, XII (Oct., 1888), 337–352.

SIMON, OLIVER, BEATRICE WARDE, AND JULIUS RODENBERG. *Printing of To-day, an Illustrated Survey of Post-War Typography in Europe and the United States.* London: P. Davies, 1928.

SOULE, GEORGE. *Prosperity Decade: From War to Depression: 1917–1929.* New York: Rinehart, 1947.

STYLUS [pseud. of William Loy]. "Bosqui Engraving and Printing Company," *Inland Printer*, XVIII (Nov., 1896), 187.

——. "C. A. Murdock & Co., San Francisco," *Inland Printer*, XVIII (Oct., 1896), 63.

——. "Cubery & Company, Printers, San Francisco," *Inland Printer*, XX (Dec., 1897), 339.

——. "Edward C. Hughes, Printer, San Francisco," *Inland Printer*, XIX (June, 1897), 302.

——. "The Francis-Valentine Company, San Francisco," *Inland Printer*, XVIII (March, 1897), 679.

——. "Franklin Printing Office, San Francisco," *Inland Printer*, XVIII (Dec., 1896), 317.

——. "John Monahan & Co., San Francisco," *Inland Printer*, XX (Nov., 1897), 195.

——. "Louis Roesch Company, San Francisco," *Inland Printer*, XIX (Aug., 1897), 547.

——. "P. J. Thomas, Printer and Journalist, San Francisco," *Inland Printer*, XIX (July, 1897), 441.

——. "The Schmidt Label & Lithographing Company, San Francisco," *Inland Printer*, XIX (Apr., 1897), 52–53.

——. "Sterett Printing Company, San Francisco," *Inland Printer*, XX (Oct., 1897), 61.

——. "Upton Brothers, Printers, San Francisco," *Inland Printer*, XIX (Sept., 1897), 667.

——. "Walter N. Brunt, San Francisco," *Inland Printer*, XIX (May, 1897), 185–186.

——. "Winterburn & Co., San Francisco," *Inland Printer*, XVIII (Jan., 1897), 426.

SWANBERG, W. A. *Citizen Hearst, a Biography*. New York: C. Scribner's Sons, 1961.

THOMPSON, PAUL. *The Work of William Morris*. New York: Viking Press, 1967.

TODD, FRANK MORTON. *The Story of the Exposition*. New York: Putnam's Sons, 1921. 5 vols.

TYLER, FRANCES W. "Some Notes of a Bookman," *Impressions Annual*, I (1911/12) 1–2.

WAGNER, HENRY R. "Commercial Printers of San Francisco from 1851 to 1880," Bibliographical Society of America, *Papers*, XXXIII (1939), 69–84.

———. "Edward Bosqui, Printer and Man of Affairs," *California Historical Society Quarterly*, XXI (Dec., 1942), 321–332.

WALTER, FRANKLIN. *San Francisco's Literary Frontier*. New York: A. A. Knopf, 1963.

William Andrews Clark Memorial Library. *Report of the First Decade, 1934–1944*. Los Angeles: University of California Press, 1946.

WILSON, KATHERINE. "Something for Beauty Here: An Account of the Ideals and Achievements of John Henry Nash, Printer," *California Arts and Architecture*, XXXIX (Oct., 1930), 30–32, 68.

WOLF, EDWIN, AND JOHN J. FLEMING. *Rosenbach, a Biography*. Cleveland: World Publishing Co., 1960.

NEWSPAPERS

Newspapers were not systematically searched because Nash subscribed to a clipping service from the early Twenties to the time of his retirement. It can be assumed that most of the items about Nash appearing in newspapers were retrieved by this service. For specific references in newspapers, see the notes accompanying the text.

OTHER PERIODICAL PUBLICATIONS

The clipping service to which Nash subscribed scanned selected periodical publications other than newspapers. The notes to the text contain specific references found therein. However, the periodicals listed below proved to be such valuable sources of background information that they were systematically searched for the years specified.

American Institute of Graphic Arts. *Fifty Books of the Year*, 1923–1942.

American Printer, July, 1885–Aug., 1947.

Ars Typographica, Spring, 1918–Autumn, 1934.

Book Club of California. *Quarterly News-Letter*, May, 1933–Winter, 1947.

Book Lover, a Magazine of Book Lore, 1899–1902.

Graphic Arts and Crafts Yearbook, 1907–1913/14.

Impressions, Sept., 1900–Dec., 1901.

Impressions Annual, 1911/12.

Impressions Quarterly, 1902–1905.

The Informant, 1918–1939. Only those copies in the *Nash Archives* were searched. The publishing history of this work is rather obscure, and its beginning and terminal dates are unknown to the writer.

Inland Printer, Oct., 1883–July, 1947.

Pacific Printer and Publisher, June, 1908–June, 1947.

Personal Impressions, March–August, 1900.

Photo-Engravers Bulletin, 1911–1942.

The Pi-Box, 1923–1936. Only those copies in the *Nash Archives* were searched.

Printing Art, 1903–1941.

San Franciscan, Nov., 1926–Sept., 1931.

TNT Imprint, Dec., 1914–Aug., 1915.

Western Printer, Jan. 15–Oct. 15, 1901.

DOCUMENTS

U. S. Dist. Ct. (N. D., Cal.) Crim. 5744.

——. Crim. 5750.

INDEX

JOHN HENRY NASH
The Biography of a Career

was composed and printed by
Heritage Printers, Inc., Charlotte, North Carolina,
and bound by
Mountain States Bindery, Salt Lake City, Utah.
The plates were printed by
Consolidated Printers, Berkeley, California.
The type is Janson.